On Core Mathematics

Grade 5

D1455718

HOUGHTON MIFFLIN HARCOURT

Table of Contents

Operations and Algebraic Thinking

Number and Operations in Base Ten

▶ **Perform operations with multi-digit whole numbers and with decimals to hundredths.**

Number and Operations—Fractions

▶ **Use equivalent fractions as a strategy to add and subtract fractions.**

▶ **Apply and extend previous understandings of multiplication and division to multiply and divide fractions.**

© Houghton Mifflin Harcourt Publishing Company

Measurement and Data

© Houghton Mifflin Harcourt Publishing Company

Geometry

1. Mr. Perkins used the expression $20 - 10 - 3 \times 2$ to find how much change he should receive. How much change should he receive?

   Ⓐ $2
   Ⓑ $4
   Ⓒ $6
   Ⓓ $14

2. Randy used the expression $2 \times 3 + 3 \times 6 + 1$ to find the number of points the Jaguars scored in all. How many points did the Jaguars score in all?

   Ⓐ 25
   Ⓑ 55
   Ⓒ 73
   Ⓓ 74

3. Amanda used the expression $8 + 25 \times 2 - 45$ to find how many beads she has. How many beads does she have?

   Ⓐ 3
   Ⓑ 13
   Ⓒ 21
   Ⓓ 103

4. Arlene used the expression $3 \times 6 + 2 \times 8 + 1$ to find the number of drinks she bought altogether. How many drinks did she buy altogether?

   Ⓐ 215
   Ⓑ 195
   Ⓒ 36
   Ⓓ 35

5. Brett evaluated the expression $5 + 12 \times 3 + 15 \times 2$ to find the total cost of some CDs. He says the total cost is $81. Explain the error that Brett made and find the correct total cost.

   _____
   _____
   _____
   _____

1. Meredith and her brother Liam are saving to buy a basketball hoop that costs $75. Meredith earns $15 per week for babysitting and spends $6 of it. Liam earns $10 per week for walking dogs and spends $4 of it. Which expression can be used to find out how many weeks it will take to save for the basketball hoop?

   Ⓐ $75 \div [(15 - 6) + (10 - 4)]$
   Ⓑ $75 \div [(15 + 6) - (10 + 4)]$
   Ⓒ $75 \div [(15 - 6) + (10 + 4)]$
   Ⓓ $75 \div [(15 - 6) - (10 - 4)]$

2. A hotel costs $89 per night. Sally will receive a $5 per night discount for paying in advance. A rental car costs $35 per day plus taxes that total $4 per day. Which expression can Sally use to find how much she will pay for the hotel and rental car for 5 days?

   Ⓐ $5 \times (89 - 5) - (35 + 4)$
   Ⓑ $[5 \times (89 - 5)] + (35 + 4)$
   Ⓒ $5 \times [(89 - 5) - (35 + 4)]$
   Ⓓ $5 \times [(89 - 5) + (35 + 4)]$

3. Of the 90 trading cards Yoshi has, 55 are baseball cards and 35 are football cards. He gives Henry 10 football cards and Henry gives Yoshi 8 baseball cards. Which expression can be used to find the number of trading cards Yoshi has now?

   Ⓐ $(55 + 8) - (35 + 10)$
   Ⓑ $(55 - 8) - (35 + 10)$
   Ⓒ $(55 - 8) + (35 - 10)$
   Ⓓ $(55 + 8) + (35 - 10)$

4. Jonah is a baker. Each morning, he makes 60 cupcakes. He gives away 5 and sells the rest. Each morning, he also makes 48 brownies. He gives away 4 and sells the rest. Which expression can be used to find how many cupcakes and brownies Jonah sells in 7 days?

   Ⓐ $7 \times [(60 - 5) - (48 - 4)]$
   Ⓑ $7 \times [(60 - 5) + (48 - 4)]$
   Ⓒ $[7 \times (60 - 5)] + (48 - 4)$
   Ⓓ $7 \times (60 - 5) + (48 - 4)$

5. Evaluate the expression $2 \times [(25 + 3) + (15 - 2)]$. Explain your work.

   _____

   _____

   _____

   _____

   _____

Operations and Algebraic Thinking

1. Jamie baked 24 cupcakes. Her sister Mia ate 3 cupcakes, and her brother David ate 2 cupcakes. Which expression can Jamie use to find how many cupcakes are left?

   (A) $24 + (3 - 2)$

   (B) $24 - (3 + 2)$

   (C) $(24 - 3) + 2$

   (D) $24 - (3 - 2)$

2. Paul displays his sports trophies on shelves in his room. He has 5 trophies on each of 3 shelves and 2 trophies on another shelf. Which expression could Paul use to find the total number of trophies displayed?

   (A) $(5 \times 3) - 2$

   (B) $5 \times (3 + 2)$

   (C) $5 + (3 \times 2)$

   (D) $(5 \times 3) + 2$

3. William won 50 tickets at the arcade. He redeemed 30 tickets for a prize and gave 5 tickets to Katelyn. Which expression can William use to find how many tickets he has left?

   (A) $50 - (30 + 5)$

   (B) $50 + (30 - 5)$

   (C) $(50 + 30) + 5$

   (D) $50 - (30 - 5)$

4. Rupal poured muffin batter into 3 muffin tins. Each muffin tin holds 8 muffins. She kept 6 muffins and took the rest to school for the bake sale. Which expression could be used to find the total number of muffins Rupal took to school for the bake sale?

   (A) $(3 \times 8) + 6$

   (B) $(3 + 8) - 6$

   (C) $(3 \times 8) - 6$

   (D) $3 \times (8 - 6)$

5. There are 12 apartments on each floor of a building. All but 3 apartments on each floor have one bedroom. The building has 4 floors. Explain how you could write an expression to find the number of one-bedroom apartments in the building.

   _____

   _____

   _____

   _____

   _____

Operations and Algebraic Thinking

Use the table for 1–2.

Jawan made a table to figure out how much he earns at his job.

Job Earnings

Days	1	2	3	4
Hours Worked	6	12	18	24
Amount Earned ($)	54	108	162	216

1. What rule relates the hours worked to the amount earned?

   Ⓐ Add 6.   © Multiply by 2.

   Ⓑ Add 54.   Ⓓ Multiply by 9.

2. Suppose Jawan works 6 days. Using the rule that relates the hours worked to the amount earned, find the total number of hours he will work in 6 days and how much money he will earn in all.

   Ⓐ 36 hours, $648

   Ⓑ 36 hours, $324

   © 30 hours, $300

   Ⓓ 30 hours, $270

3. What is the unknown number in Sequence 2 in the chart?

Sequence Number	1	2	3	5	7
Sequence 1	3	6	9	15	21
Sequence 2	15	30	45	75	?

   Ⓐ 63   © 105

   Ⓑ 90   Ⓓ 150

4. Wanda made a table to show the number of ounces of flour she uses to make cupcakes.

Flour in Cupcakes

Batches	1	2	3	4	6
Ounces of Flour	8	16	24	32	48
Cupcakes	16	32	48	64	96

   What rule relates the number of ounces of flour to the number of cupcakes?

   Ⓐ Add 8.   © Multiply by 2.

   Ⓑ Add 12.   Ⓓ Multiply by 8.

5. Mrs. Marston determined how many tubes of paint she would need for the students in her art classes to complete their projects. How many tubes of paint will she need for the class with 20 students? Explain how you found the answer.

Students	4	8	12	16	20
Tubes	8	16	24	32	

_____

_____

Operations and Algebraic Thinking

1. Nomi is making a pattern of square tiles, as shown below. The side lengths of the tiles are 2 centimeters.

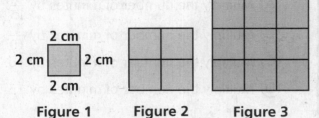

| Figure 1 | Figure 2 | Figure 3 |

Suppose Nomi continues the pattern. What will be the distance around Figure 7?

Ⓐ 14 centimeters

Ⓑ 49 centimeters

Ⓒ 56 centimeters

Ⓓ 98 centimeters

2. Leroy starts to work at a part-time job. He saves $25 of his earnings each month. By the end of the second month, he saves $50 in all. How much will he save by the end of 24 months?

Ⓐ $75   Ⓒ $1,200

Ⓑ $600   Ⓓ $1,800

Use the table for 3–4.

The table shows the number of tickets needed for rides at an amusement park.

Amusement Park Rides

Number of Rides	1	2	3	7
Number of Tickets	4	8	12	?

3. Which rule relates the number of tickets to the number of rides?

Ⓐ Multiply the number of rides by 4.

Ⓑ Multiply the number of rides by 3.

Ⓒ Add 3 for each ride.

Ⓓ Add 4 for each ride.

4. Jared buys 40 tickets and goes on 7 rides. How many tickets does he have left after the 7 rides?

Ⓐ 33   Ⓒ 24

Ⓑ 28   Ⓓ 12

5. A restaurant manager has 10 tables that are 3 feet wide and 4 feet long. Suppose the manager places the 10 tables side-by-side so the 4-foot sides match up. What will be the perimeter of the larger table that is formed? Explain how you know.

3 ft

4 ft

_____

_____

_____

_____

Use the graph for 1–3.

The graph shows the relationship between the time and the number of push ups Eric did.

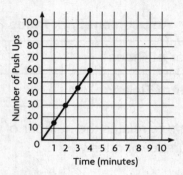

1. What is the total number of push ups Eric did in 3 minutes?

   (A) 40   (C) 50

   (B) 45   (D) 55

2. What rule relates the number of push ups to the time?

   (A) Multiply the number of minutes by $\frac{1}{15}$.

   (B) Multiply the number of minutes by $\frac{1}{10}$.

   (C) Multiply the number of minutes by 10.

   (D) Multiply the number of minutes by 15.

3. Suppose Eric continues to do push ups at this rate. What is the total number of push ups he will do in 5 minutes?

   (A) 50   (C) 75

   (B) 65   (D) 90

4. Randy makes a table that shows how long it takes her to run different distances.

Running Time and Distance

Number of miles	1	2	3	4
Time (in minutes)	10	20	30	40

Draw a line graph to show the relationship between the number of miles and the time. Explain how you can use the graph to find how long it will take Randy to run 5 miles at the same rate.

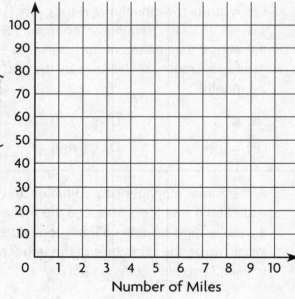

_____

_____

_____

_____

1. A math workbook contains 50 pages. The number of problems in the book is 10 times as many as the number of pages. How many problems are in the math workbook?

   (A)   5

   (B)   500

   (C) 5,000

   (D) 50,000

2. Cara has saved $4,000 to buy a car. Rick wants to buy a new television set. He has saved $\frac{1}{10}$ as much as Cara. How much has Rick saved?

   (A) $4

   (B) $40

   (C) $400

   (D) $40,000

3. Riva lives 300 miles from her grandparents. George lives 10 times that distance from his grandparents. How many miles does George live from his grandparents?

   (A)   30

   (B)   3,000

   (C) 30,000

   (D) 300,000

4. The Davis family pays $200,000 for a new house. They make a down payment that is $\frac{1}{10}$ of the price of the house. How much is the down payment?

   (A) $20

   (B) $200

   (C) $2,000

   (D) $20,000

5. Joshua earns $60,000 a year at his job. He is getting a raise that is $\frac{1}{10}$ of the amount he earns now. Joshua says that his new salary will be $60,600. Do you agree? Support your answer.

   _____

   _____

   _____

   _____

   _____

1. A publisher reports that it sold 2,419,386 children's magazines. What is the value of the digit 2 in 2,419,386?

   Ⓐ 200,000,000

   Ⓑ 20,000,000

   Ⓒ 2,000,000

   Ⓓ 200,000

2. The diameter of Saturn at its equator is about 120,540,000 meters. What is 120,540,000 written in word form?

   Ⓐ twelve thousand, five hundred forty

   Ⓑ twelve million, five hundred forty thousand

   Ⓒ one hundred twenty million, fifty-four thousand

   Ⓓ one hundred twenty million, five hundred forty thousand

3. A printing company used 1,896,432 sheets of tag board last year. What is the value of the digit 8 in 1,896,432?

   Ⓐ 800

   Ⓑ 8,000

   Ⓒ 80,000

   Ⓓ 800,000

4. A company manufactured forty-eight million, seven hundred fifty thousand toothpicks last month. What is this number written in standard form?

   Ⓐ 48,750,000

   Ⓑ 48,700,050

   Ⓒ 48,000,750

   Ⓓ 48,750

5. Rayna lives in Fulton, which has a population of 260,980 people. Rayna wrote 260,980 as $(2 \times 100,000) + (6 \times 10,000) + (9 \times 1,000) + (8 \times 100)$. What error did Rayna make? Write the correct expanded form.

_____

_____

_____

_____

_____

_____

_____

_____

Number and Operations in Base Ten

1. A calculator is 0.07 meter wide. Sam made a model that was $\frac{1}{10}$ the size of the actual calculator. How wide was Sam's model?

   Ⓐ 70 meters

   Ⓑ 7 meters

   Ⓒ 0.7 meter

   Ⓓ 0.007 meter

2. A word in a book is 0.009 meter long. Kai looked at the word with a lens that made it look 10 times as large as the actual word. How long did the word look?

   Ⓐ 0.0009 meter

   Ⓑ 0.09 meter

   Ⓒ 0.9 meter

   Ⓓ 9 meters

3. What is the relationship between 0.008 and 0.08?

   Ⓐ 0.008 is $\frac{1}{10}$ of 0.08.

   Ⓑ 0.08 is $\frac{1}{10}$ of 0.008.

   Ⓒ 0.008 is 10 times as much as 0.08.

   Ⓓ 0.008 is equal to 0.08.

4. Valerie made a model for a decimal. What decimal is shown by Valerie's model?

   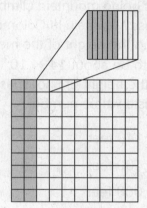

   Ⓐ 0.026   Ⓒ 0.216

   Ⓑ 0.206   Ⓓ 0.26

5. A jeweler used 0.5 ounce of gold to make a necklace. He used $\frac{1}{10}$ as much gold in an earring. Explain how to use place-value patterns to find how much gold the jeweler used in the earring.

   _____

   _____

   _____

   _____

1. A Coast Guard ship is responsible for searching an area that is 5,000 square miles. Which shows 5,000 as a whole number multiplied by a power of ten?

   Ⓐ 5×10^1
   Ⓑ 5×10^2
   Ⓒ 5×10^3
   Ⓓ 5×10^4

2. Martin is going mountain climbing at Snowmass Mountain in Colorado. He looked up the height of the mountain and found it to be about 14×10^3 feet high. What is the height of Snowmass Mountain written as a whole number?

   Ⓐ   140 feet
   Ⓑ   1,400 feet
   Ⓒ 14,000 feet
   Ⓓ 140,000 feet

3. Patel hopes to be one of the first fans to get into the stadium for the baseball game because the first 30,000 fans will receive a baseball cap. Which shows 30,000 as a whole number multiplied by a power of ten?

   Ⓐ 3×10^1
   Ⓑ 3×10^2
   Ⓒ 3×10^3
   Ⓓ 3×10^4

4. Trisha is writing a report about Guam for Social Studies. She looked up the population of Guam and found it to be about 18×10^4. What is the population of Guam written as a whole number?

   Ⓐ 180,000
   Ⓑ 18,000
   Ⓒ   1,800
   Ⓓ   180

5. June wrote an essay on saving energy for a contest. She won a $5,000 scholarship. Explain how June can write $5,000 as a whole number multiplied by a power of ten in two different ways.

   _____

   _____

   _____

   _____

   _____

   _____

   _____

1. A country music concert will be held at a local park. The promoters have already sold 3,000 concert tickets. Each ticket costs $20. How much money have the promoters already collected?

   Ⓐ $60
   Ⓑ $600
   Ⓒ $60,000
   Ⓓ $600,000

2. Clinton decided to buy 300 shares of stock in an electronics company. Each share costs $60. Which of the following could he use to find the total amount he will pay for the stock?

   Ⓐ $(6 \times 3) \times 10^2 = 1,800$
   Ⓑ $(6 \times 3) \times 10^3 = 18,000$
   Ⓒ $(6 \times 3) \times 10^4 = 180,000$
   Ⓓ $(6 \times 3) \times 10^5 = 1,800,000$

3. Sam is using a microscope to look at a plant specimen. The microscope magnifies the specimen 4×10^2 times. If the specimen is 3 centimeters long, how long will the magnified specimen appear to be?

   Ⓐ   70 centimeters
   Ⓑ   120 centimeters
   Ⓒ   700 centimeters
   Ⓓ 1,200 centimeters

4. So far the fifth-grade students at Silver Run Elementary School have raised $200 toward their class trip. They need to raise 8 times as much to pay for the whole trip. How much money do the fifth-grade students need to raise in all?

   Ⓐ $16
   Ⓑ $1,600
   Ⓒ $16,000
   Ⓓ $160,000

5. The Yukon River in British Columbia is about 4 times as long as the Osage River in Kansas. If the Osage River is 5×10^2 miles long, about how long is the Yukon River? Explain how you found your answer.

   _____

   _____

   _____

   _____

   _____

   _____

1. Ganesh is making a scale model of the Space Needle in Seattle, Washington, for a report on the state of Washington. The Space Needle is 605 feet tall. If the model is $\frac{1}{100}$ of the actual size of the Space Needle, how tall is the model?

   (A) 0.605 foot

   (B) 6.05 feet

   (C) 6.5 feet

   (D) 60.5 feet

2. Madison needs to buy enough meat to make 1,000 hamburgers for the company picnic. Each hamburger will weigh 0.25 pound. How many pounds of hamburger meat should Madison buy?

   (A) 2.5 pounds

   (B) 25 pounds

   (C) 250 pounds

   (D) 2,500 pounds

3. Kareem was doing research for a report about the longest rivers on Earth. He read that the Nile River is 4.16×10^3 miles long. How should Kareem write the length of the Nile River in standard form on his report?

   (A) 4.16 miles

   (B) 41.6 miles

   (C) 416 miles

   (D) 4,160 miles

4. The school store expects to sell a lot of sweatshirts because the football team won the championship. The store ordered 100 sweatshirts. Each sweatshirt cost $8.95. How much did the order of sweatshirts cost the store?

   (A) $89.50

   (B) $895

   (C) $8,950

   (D) $89,500

5. Nathan put 0.35 quart of concentrated liquid cleaner in a bucket. Then he put 10 times that amount of water in the bucket. Nathan says he added 35 quarts of water to the bucket. Do you agree? Support your answer.

   _____

   _____

   _____

   _____

   _____

1. Lori is running in a marathon, which is 26.2 miles long. So far, she has run one-tenth of the marathon. How far has Lori run?

   (A) 262 miles

   (B) 2.62 miles

   (C) 0.262 mile

   (D) 0.00262 mile

2. A school bought 1,000 erasers as part of an order for supplies. The total cost of the erasers was $30. What was the cost of 1 eraser?

   (A) $0.03

   (B) $0.30

   (C) $300

   (D) $3,000

3. Tanya baked 100 cupcakes one morning in a bakery. She used 64 ounces of frosting to decorate the cupcakes. If each cupcake had the same amount of frosting, how much frosting did Tanya put on each cupcake?

   (A) 0.0064 ounce

   (B) 0.064 ounce

   (C) 0.64 ounce

   (D) 6.4 ounces

4. A counselor at Sleepy Hollow Camp has 225 yards of lanyard to give to 100 campers to make lanyard key chains. Each camper will get the same amount of lanyard. How much lanyard will each camper get?

   (A) 0.0225 yard

   (B) 0.225 yard

   (C) 2.25 yards

   (D) 22.5 yards

5. Thomas paid $50 for a box of multicolor file folders for his office. There were 100 folders in the box. He said that the cost of each folder was $0.05. Do you agree? Support your answer.

   _____

   _____

   _____

   _____

   _____

1. A scientist measured a grain of sand. It had a diameter of 0.049 millimeter. What is 0.049 written in word form?

Ⓐ forty-nine

Ⓑ forty-nine tenths

Ⓒ forty-nine hundredths

Ⓓ forty-nine thousandths

2. The diamond in Alma's necklace weighs 0.258 carat. What digit is in the hundredths place of 0.258?

Ⓐ 0

Ⓑ 2

Ⓒ 5

Ⓓ 8

3. The mass of an ant is about 0.003 gram. What is the value of the digit 3 in 0.003?

Ⓐ 3 ones

Ⓑ 3 tenths

Ⓒ 3 hundredths

Ⓓ 3 thousandths

4. A penny has a diameter of 0.019 meter. What is 0.019 written in word form?

Ⓐ nineteen thousandths

Ⓑ nineteen hundredths

Ⓒ nineteen tenths

Ⓓ nineteen

5. Zeke wrote the number six and fifty-eight thousandths as 6.58. Describe Zeke's error and tell how you would correct it.

_____

_____

_____

_____

Number and Operations in Base Ten

1. Harry kept a record of how far he ran each day last week.

Day	Distance (in miles)
Monday	4.5
Tuesday	3.9
Wednesday	4.25
Thursday	3.75
Friday	4.2

On which day did Harry run the greatest number of miles?

(A) Monday

(B) Tuesday

(C) Thursday

(D) Friday

2. The four highest scores on the floor exercise at a gymnastics meet were 9.675, 9.25, 9.325, and 9.5. Which shows the order of the scores from least to greatest?

(A) 9.5, 9.25, 9.325, 9.675

(B) 9.25, 9.5, 9.325, 9.675

(C) 9.675, 9.5, 9.325, 9.25

(D) 9.25, 9.325, 9.5, 9.675

3. The table shows the fastest times for the 100-meter hurdles event.

Name	Times (in seconds)
Shakira	15.45
Jameel	15.09
Lindsay	15.6
Nicholas	15.3

Who had the fastest time?

(A) Shakira   (C) Lindsay

(B) Jameel   (D) Nicholas

4. Mary Ann kept a record of how long she practiced the piano each week for a month.

Week	Hours Practiced
Week 1	4.75
Week 2	4.5
Week 3	5.1
Week 4	5.75

During which week did Mary Ann practice the greatest amount of time?

(A) Week 1   (C) Week 3

(B) Week 2   (D) Week 4

5. In a balance beam event, Eva scored 9.375 points and Yuko scored 9.325 points. How should Eva and Yuko compare their scores to find who had the greater score? Explain your answer.

_____

_____

_____

_____

1. It takes the dwarf planet Pluto 247.68 years to revolve once around the sun. What is 247.68 years rounded to the nearest whole number of years?

    (A) 247 years

    (B) 247.6 years

    (C) 247.7 years

    (D) 248 years

2. The flagpole in front of Silver Pines Elementary School is 18.375 feet tall. What is 18.375 rounded to the nearest tenth?

    (A) 18

    (B) 18.38

    (C) 18.4

    (D) 20

3. Michelle records the value of one Euro in U.S. dollars each day for her social studies project. The table shows the data she has recorded so far.

Day	Value of 1 Euro (In U.S. dollars)
Monday	1.448
Tuesday	1.443
Wednesday	1.452
Thursday	1.458

    On which day does the value of 1 Euro round to $1.46 to the nearest hundredth?

    (A) Monday   (C) Wednesday

    (B) Tuesday   (D) Thursday

4. Jackie found a rock that has a mass of 78.852 grams. What is the mass of the rock rounded to the nearest tenth?

    (A) 78.85 grams   (C) 79 grams

    (B) 78.9 grams   (D) 80 grams

5. It takes the planet Neptune about 164.8 years to revolve once around the sun. What are the least and greatest numbers written in hundredths that could round to 164.8? Explain your answer.

    _____

    _____

    _____

    _____

    _____

Number and Operations in Base Ten

1. A bus driver travels 234 miles every day. How many miles does the bus driver travel in 5 days?

   (A) 1,050 miles

   (B) 1,150 miles

   (C) 1,170 miles

   (D) 1,520 miles

2. Hector does 165 sit-ups every day. How many sit-ups does he do in 7 days?

   (A) 1,155

   (B) 1,145

   (C) 1,125

   (D) 725

3. Lara and Chad are both saving to buy cars. So far, Chad has saved $1,235. Lara has saved 5 times as much as Chad. How much has Lara saved?

   (A) $5,055

   (B) $6,055

   (C) $6,075

   (D) $6,175

4. Mavis drives 634 miles to visit her grandmother in Philadelphia. How many miles does Mavis drive if she visits her grandmother 4 times?

   (A) 2,426 miles

   (B) 2,436 miles

   (C) 2,536 miles

   (D) 2,836 miles

5. Cheryl and Richard decided to spend 5 months a year in Florida. The rent for the apartment they like is $885 per month. Cheryl said the total rent would be $40,425. Richard said the total rent would be $4,425. Explain how you can use an estimate to determine who is correct.

   _____

   _____

   _____

   _____

   _____

   _____

   _____

   _____

1. Chen burns 354 calories in 1 hour swimming. He swam for 28 hours last month. How many calories did Chen burn in all last month from swimming?

   (A) 3,010 calories

   (B) 8,482 calories

   (C) 9,912 calories

   (D) 10,266 calories

2. Rachel earns $27 per hour at work. She worked 936 hours last year. How much did Rachel earn working last year?

   (A) $7,584

   (B) $24,932

   (C) $25,272

   (D) $25,332

3. A company manufactures 295 toy cars each day. How many toy cars do they manufacture in 34 days?

   (A) 3,065

   (B) 7,610

   (C) 10,065

   (D) 10,030

4. Raul earns $24 per hour painting houses. If he works for 263 hours, how much will Raul earn in all?

   (A) $6,312

   (B) $6,112

   (C) $5,102

   (D) $1,578

5. Last year, Danielle worked 35 hours a week in a bookstore and earned $11 an hour. Danielle says that she earned about $20,000 last year. Do you agree? Support your answer with information from the problem.

   _____

   _____

   _____

   _____

   _____

   _____

   _____

   _____

1. Sherry's family is going to a beach resort. Sherry bought 7 beach towels that cost $13 each to take to the resort. To find the total cost, she added the products of 7×10 and 7×3, for a total of $91. What property did Sherry use?

   (A) Commutative Property of Multiplication

   (B) Commutative Property of Addition

   (C) Associative Property of Multiplication

   (D) Distributive Property

2. Chen bought a basketball for $23, a pair of running shoes for $35, and a baseball cap for $7. He wrote the equation $23 + 35 + 7 = 23 + 7 + 35$. What property did Chen use?

   (A) Associative Property of Addition

   (B) Commutative Property of Addition

   (C) Distributive Property

   (D) Identity Property of Multiplication

3. Nicole baked 9 trays of cookies. Each tray had 5 rows with 4 cookies in each row. Nicole wrote the equation $(9 \times 5) \times 4 = 9 \times (5 \times 4)$. What property did Nicole use?

   (A) Commutative Property of Multiplication

   (B) Associative Property of Addition

   (C) Associative Property of Multiplication

   (D) Distributive Property

4. Ramon has a large collection of marbles. He has 150 clear marbles, 214 blue marbles, and 89 green marbles. Ramon wrote this equation about his marble collection:

   $(150 + 214) + 89 = 150 + (214 + 89)$

   What property did Ramon use?

   (A) Associative Property of Addition

   (B) Commutative Property of Addition

   (C) Identity Property of Addition

   (D) Distributive Property

5. Allison and Justin's father donated $3 for every lap they swam in a swim-a-thon. Allison swam 21 laps and Justin swam 15 laps. Use the Distributive Property to find the amount of money their father donated.

   _____

   _____

   _____

   _____

   _____

1. Francine took 42 photos with her digital camera. She stored an equal number of photos in each of 3 folders on her computer. Which multiplication sentence could Francine use to find the number of photos in each folder?

Ⓐ $3 \times 14 = 42$

Ⓑ $3 \times 40 = 120$

Ⓒ $3 \times 42 = 126$

Ⓓ $4 \times 42 = 168$

2. Amber baked 120 cookies to give to 5 friends. She wants to put the same number of cookies in each bag. Which of the following can she use to find how many cookies to put in each bag?

Ⓐ $(5 \times 20) + (5 \times 4)$

Ⓑ $(5 \times 10) + (5 \times 8)$

Ⓒ $(5 \times 60) + (5 \times 2)$

Ⓓ $(5 \times 15) + (5 \times 5)$

3. Shari sent a total of 64 text messages to 4 friends. Each friend received the same number of text messages. Which multiplication sentence could Shari use to find the number of text messages she sent to each friend?

Ⓐ $4 \times 64 = 256$

Ⓑ $60 \times 4 = 240$

Ⓒ $5 \times 64 = 320$

Ⓓ $4 \times 16 = 64$

4. Jared has 96 books to arrange on 6 shelves of a bookcase. He wants each shelf to have the same number of books. Which of the following **cannot** be used to find how many books Jared can put on each shelf?

Ⓐ $(6 \times 10) + (6 \times 6)$

Ⓑ $(6 \times 8) + (6 \times 8)$

Ⓒ $(6 \times 4) + (6 \times 4)$

Ⓓ $(6 \times 15) + (6 \times 1)$

5. Lee has 72 photos to put into a photo album. He can put 3 photos on each page. Explain how Lee can use the Distributive Property to divide and find the number of pages he will use in the album.

_____

_____

_____

_____

_____

Number and Operations in Base Ten

1. Marta has 16 postcards from each of 8 different cities in Pennsylvania. She can fit 4 postcards on each page of her scrapbook. How many pages in the scrapbook can Marta fill with postcards?

   (A) 32
   (B) 41
   (C) 128
   (D) 512

2. Nathan's orchestra has 18 string musicians, 9 percussion musicians, 15 brass musicians, and 12 woodwind musicians. Six of the musicians cannot play in the next performance. If the remaining musicians plan to sit in rows of 6 chairs, how many rows of chairs are needed?

   (A) 4
   (B) 6
   (C) 8
   (D) 9

3. There are 6 buses transporting students to a baseball game, with 32 students on each bus. Each row at the baseball stadium seats 8 students. If the students fill up all of the rows, how many rows of seats will the students need altogether?

   (A) 22
   (B) 23
   (C) 24
   (D) 1,536

4. Laura has 24 stamps from each of 6 different countries. She can fit 4 stamps on each display sheet of an album. How many display sheets can Laura fill with stamps?

   (A) 576
   (B) 36
   (C) 34
   (D) 16

5. Ming's DVD collection includes 16 adventure movies, 7 comedies, 12 westerns, and 8 mysteries. He wants to keep 2 of each type of DVD and give away the rest. Ming says that if he gives an equal number of DVDs to 5 friends, he will give each friend 7 DVDs. Do you agree? Support your answer.

   _____

   _____

   _____

   _____

   _____

1. Caleb needs to solve the problem
   2,406 ÷ 6. In what place is the first
   digit of the quotient for the problem
   2,406 ÷ 6?

   (A) ones   (C) hundreds

   (B) tens   (D) thousands

2. Mrs. Tao has 154 books on 7 shelves in her
   classroom. Each shelf has the same number
   of books on it. She wants to find out the
   number of books on each shelf. In what place
   should Mrs. Tao write the first digit of the
   quotient for the problem 154 ÷ 7?

   (A) ones   (C) hundreds

   (B) tens   (D) thousands

3. The last problem on Jacob's math test was
   9,072 ÷ 9. In what place should Jacob
   write the first digit of the quotient for the
   problem 9,072 ÷ 9?

   (A) ones   (C) hundreds

   (B) tens   (D) thousands

4. Raul has 486 baseball cards in 9 albums.
   Each album has the same number of
   baseball cards. He wants to find the
   number of baseball cards in each album.
   In what place should Raul write the first
   digit of the quotient for the problem
   486 ÷ 9?

   (A) ones   (C) hundreds

   (B) tens   (D) thousands

5. Elizabeth was assigned the problem 3,402 ÷ 6 for homework. Explain
   how Elizabeth could use place value to write the first digit in the quotient
   of 3,402 ÷ 6.

   _____

   _____

   _____

   _____

   _____

1. During a school fund raiser, the fifth-grade classes sold rolls of wrapping paper. The table shows how many rolls each class sold. The rolls were sold in packages of 4.

Wrapping Paper Sold

Class	Total Rolls
Ms. Lane	672
Mr. Milner	184
Mrs. Jackson	228

How many packages of wrapping paper did Ms. Lane's class sell?

Ⓐ 2,688 Ⓒ 168
Ⓑ 173 Ⓓ 143

2. Sophia wants to buy collector boxes that can hold 6 dolls each. How many boxes will Sophia need to buy for her collection of 168 dolls?

Ⓐ 21 Ⓒ 34
Ⓑ 28 Ⓓ 1,008

3. On a standard week-long space shuttle flight, 175 servings of fresh food are shared equally among 7 crewmembers. How many servings of fresh food does each crewmember receive?

Ⓐ 25 Ⓒ 32
Ⓑ 26 Ⓓ 33

4. A bakery sold croissants to local restaurants. The table shows how many croissants were sold to each restaurant. The croissants were sold 6 to a box.

Croissants Sold

Restaurant	Number of Croissants
The Coffee Counter	546
La Claudette	768
Bon Jour	858

How many boxes of croissants did the bakery sell to La Claudette?

Ⓐ 4,608 Ⓒ 128
Ⓑ 143 Ⓓ 96

5. Avery made mosaic tile trays for a craft fair. He used 4,072 tiles to make 8 trays. Each tray had the same number of tiles. Avery made a display saying that he used 59 tiles for each tray. Was Avery's sign correct? Support your answer with information from the problem.

_____

_____

_____

_____

1. Emma used a quick picture to help her divide 154 by 11. What is the quotient?

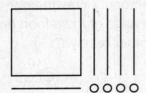

(A) 11   (C) 13

(B) 12   (D) 14

2. Garrett used a quick picture to help him divide 182 by 14. What is the quotient?

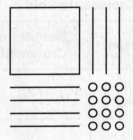

(A) 11   (C) 13

(B) 12   (D) 14

3. Latoya drew a quick picture to solve a division problem. Which division problem does the quick picture show?

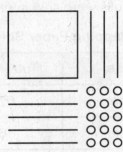

(A) $195 \div 15 = 13$

(B) $169 \div 13 = 13$

(C) $180 \div 15 = 12$

(D) $165 \div 15 = 11$

4. Ling has 168 baseball cards. He put the same number of cards into each of 14 piles. How many baseball cards did Ling put in each pile?

(A) 11   (C) 13

(B) 12   (D) 14

5. Nick has 192 stickers. He buys a new sticker album and will put 16 stickers on each page of the album. Explain how Nick can use base-ten blocks to find how many full pages of stickers he will have.

_____

_____

_____

_____

Number and Operations in Base Ten

1. Jacob divided 976 by 28 using partial quotients. What is missing from Jacob's work?

$$
\begin{array}{r}
34 \ r24 \\
28\overline{)976} \\
\end{array}
$$

$$
\begin{array}{r}
-280 \quad \leftarrow 10 \times 28 \qquad 10 \\
\overline{696} \\
-280 \quad \leftarrow 10 \times 28 \qquad 10 \\
\overline{416} \\
-280 \quad \leftarrow 10 \times 28 \qquad 10 \\
\overline{136} \\
-\Box \quad \leftarrow 4 \times 28 \qquad +\ 4 \\
\overline{24} \qquad\qquad\qquad 34
\end{array}
$$

(A) 24

(C) 112

(B) 34

(D) 280

2. Orah takes an 18-day bike tour. She rides 756 miles in all. What is the average number of miles she rides each day?

(A) 32

(C) 90

(B) 42

(D) 92

3. Paloma divided 1,292 by 31 using partial quotients. What is the quotient?

$$
\begin{array}{r}
31\overline{)1,292} \\
-930 \quad \leftarrow 30 \times 31 \qquad 30 \\
\overline{362} \\
-310 \quad \leftarrow 10 \times 31 \qquad 10 \\
\overline{52} \\
-31 \quad \leftarrow 1 \times 31 \qquad +\ 1 \\
\overline{21} \qquad\qquad\qquad 41
\end{array}
$$

(A) 21

(C) 41

(B) 21 r41

(D) 41 r21

4. The school library has 2,976 books on its shelves. Each shelf has 48 books on it. How many shelves are in the library?

(A) 42

(B) 52

(C) 62

(D) 192

5. Lainie has a collection of 1,824 stamps that she wants to put into envelopes. She wants to put 48 stamps into each envelope. How many envelopes does Lainie need? Describe the steps you would follow to find the answer using partial quotients with multiples of 20.

_____

_____

_____

_____

1. Lauren bought a television that cost $805. She plans to make equal payments of $38 each month until the television is paid in full. About how many payments will Lauren make?

   (A) 20
   (B) 30
   (C) 38
   (D) 40

2. Miss Roja plans to sell tote bags at the art festival for $33 each. She will need to make $265 to pay the rent for the space at the festival. About how many tote bags will she need to sell to pay the rent?

   (A) 3
   (B) 7
   (C) 9
   (D) 30

3. Mrs. Ortega bought a dishwasher that cost $579. She will make monthly payments in the amount of $28 until the dishwasher is paid in full. About how many payments will Mrs. Ortega make?

   (A) 12
   (B) 20
   (C) 28
   (D) 30

4. Doug plans to sell mugs at the craft fair for $21 each. He will need to make $182 to pay the rent for the space at the fair. About how many mugs will he need to sell to pay the rent?

   (A) 2
   (B) 6
   (C) 9
   (D) 20

5. Henry has 1,875 photos to put in albums which hold 72 photos each. He says he needs between 20 and 30 photo albums. Do you agree with Henry? Explain your answer using compatible numbers.

   _____

   _____

   _____

   _____

   _____

   _____

1. The local concert hall has 48 concerts scheduled this season. Each concert has the same number of tickets available for sale. There is a total of 4,560 tickets. How many tickets are available for each concert?

Ⓐ 1,140

Ⓑ 950

Ⓒ 105

Ⓓ 95

2. The director of a pet shelter received a shipment of 1,110 puppy blankets. He put the same number of blankets in each of 27 boxes and put the leftover blankets in the puppy kennels. How many blankets were put in the puppy kennels?

Ⓐ 3

Ⓑ 18

Ⓒ 28

Ⓓ 41

3. An airplane has 416 seats arranged in 52 rows. If there is the same number of seats in each row, how many seats are in one row?

Ⓐ 21,632

Ⓑ 364

Ⓒ 8

Ⓓ 6

4. Mr. Stephens needs to haul 1,518 tons of rock from a construction site. His dump truck can hold 26 tons per load. How many tons will Mr. Stephens need to haul in the last load to move all of the rock?

Ⓐ 10

Ⓑ 58

Ⓒ 68

Ⓓ 1,492

5. Meagan uses shipping boxes to mail 850 bags of glass beads. Each box can hold 24 bags. Meagan says there will be 10 bags of glass beads in the last box. Explain how Meagan could have reached that conclusion.

_____

_____

_____

_____

_____

_____

1. To solve the division problem below, Kyle estimates that 2 is the first digit in the quotient.

$$29\overline{)556}$$ quotient 2, -58

Which of the following is correct?

(A) 2 is the correct first digit of the quotient.

(B) 2 is too low. The first digit should be adjusted to 4.

(C) 2 is too low. The first digit should be adjusted to 3.

(D) 2 is too high. The first digit should be adjusted to 1.

2. Alex is saving up to buy a guitar that costs $855. He plans to save $45 a month. How many months will it take him to save enough money to buy the guitar?

(A) 19 months

(B) 21 months

(C) 23 months

(D) 25 months

3. An auditorium has 1,224 seats. There are 36 seats in each row. How many rows of seats are in the auditorium?

(A) 32

(B) 34

(C) 42

(D) 44

4. Diego estimates that 3 is the first digit in the quotient of the problem below.

$$16\overline{)4272}$$ quotient 3, -48

Which of the following is correct?

(A) 3 is the correct first digit of the quotient.

(B) 3 is too low. The first digit should be adjusted to 4.

(C) 3 is too low. The first digit should be adjusted to 5.

(D) 3 is too high. The first digit should be adjusted to 2.

5. Carla is packing 768 baseball caps into boxes. She knows that 32 baseball caps will fit in each box. Carla divided the number of baseball caps by 32 to find the number of boxes she needs. She estimated and placed the first digit in the quotient.

$$32\overline{)768}$$ quotient 3

What is the next thing that Carla should do? Explain your answer.

_____

_____

_____

_____

Number and Operations in Base Ten

1. Ricardo's dog weighs 6 times as much as his cat. The total weight of his two pets is 98 pounds. How much does Ricardo's dog weigh?

   Ⓐ 92 pounds

   Ⓑ 84 pounds

   Ⓒ 16 pounds

   Ⓓ 14 pounds

2. The number of children at the library was 3 times the number of adults. The total number of people at the library was 48. How many children were at the library?

   Ⓐ 12

   Ⓑ 24

   Ⓒ 32

   Ⓓ 36

3. Sarah baby-sat 7 times as many hours during summer break as she did during spring break. She baby-sat a total of 56 hours during both breaks. How many hours did Sarah baby-sit during spring break?

   Ⓐ 49 hours

   Ⓑ 9 hours

   Ⓒ 8 hours

   Ⓓ 7 hours

4. Melanie is 3 times as old as her cousin. The total of their ages is 36 years. How old is Melanie's cousin?

   Ⓐ 9 years old

   Ⓑ 12 years old

   Ⓒ 27 years old

   Ⓓ 33 years old

5. Ian and Joe took their younger sister Michelle to pick strawberries. Ian picked 5 times as many strawberries as Michelle. Joe picked 7 times as many strawberries as Michelle. Ian and Joe picked a total of 192 strawberries. How many strawberries did Joe pick? Use a diagram to help find the answer. Explain how you used the diagram to answer the question.

   _____

   _____

   _____

   _____

   _____

   _____

   _____

1. Ken used a quick picture to model 1.77 + 1.19. Which picture shows the sum?

Ⓐ

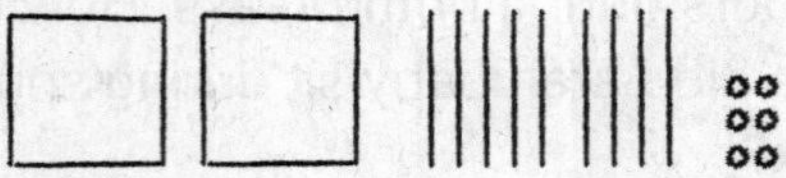

Ⓑ

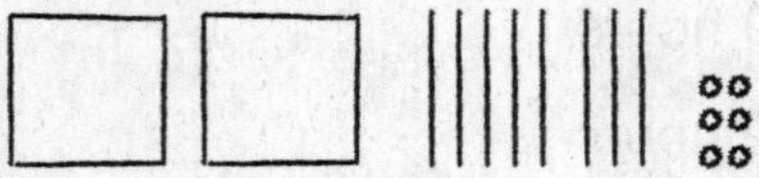

Ⓒ

Ⓓ

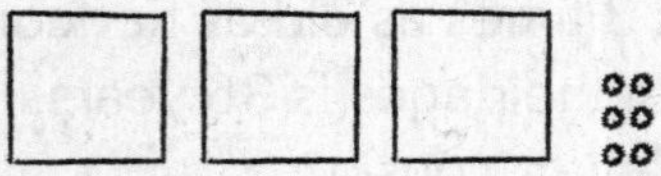

2. It took Margo 0.5 hour to do her science homework and 0.9 hour to do her math homework. How long did it take Margo to do her science and math homework?

Ⓐ 0.14 hour   Ⓒ 1.04 hours

Ⓑ 0.45 hour   Ⓓ 1.4 hours

3. It took Ray 0.45 hour to rake the leaves and 0.75 hour to mow the lawn. How long did it take Ray to rake the leaves and mow the lawn?

Ⓐ 0.12 hour   Ⓒ 1.2 hours

Ⓑ 1.1 hours   Ⓓ 1.21 hours

4. Hedy used decimal models to find the sum of 0.46 and 0.85. She drew a quick picture to represent the sum. Is Hedy correct? Explain your answer.

_____

_____

_____

_____

_____

_____

_____

Number and Operations in Base Ten

1. Taryn used a quick picture to model
2.34 − 1.47. Which picture shows the
difference?

Ⓐ

Ⓑ

Ⓒ

Ⓓ

2. Jasmine lives 1.25 miles from school and
0.82 mile from the library. How much
farther does Jasmine live from school than
from the library?

Ⓐ 0.33 mile   Ⓒ 2.07 miles

Ⓑ 0.43 mile   Ⓓ 4.3 miles

3. Avery bought 3.45 pounds of red apples
and 1.57 pounds of green apples. How
many more pounds of red apples than
green apples did Avery buy?

Ⓐ 5.02 pounds

Ⓑ 1.98 pounds

Ⓒ 1.88 pounds

Ⓓ 1.12 pounds

4. Hector used decimal models to find 1.29 − 0.64.
He drew a quick picture to represent the difference.
Is Hector correct? Explain your answer.

_____

_____

_____

_____

_____

_____

_____

_____

1. Julie has $16.73. She buys a purse that costs $4.12. About how much money will Julie have left?

   (A) $3

   (B) $13

   (C) $21

   (D) $23

2. A vet measured the mass of two birds. The mass of the robin was 76.64 grams. The mass of the blue jay was 81.54 grams. Which is the best estimate of the difference in the masses of the birds?

   (A) 5 grams

   (B) 10 grams

   (C) 15 grams

   (D) 20 grams

3. A town plans to add a 3.88-kilometer extension to a road that is currently 5.02 kilometers long. Which is the best estimate of the length of the road after the extension is added?

   (A) 1 kilometer

   (B) 2 kilometers

   (C) 4 kilometers

   (D) 9 kilometers

4. Denise has $78.22. She wants to buy a computer game that costs $29.99. About how much money will Denise have left?

   (A) $40

   (B) $50

   (C) $60

   (D) $110

5. Jennifer has $12 to spend on lunch and the roller rink. Admission to the roller rink is $5.75. Jennifer estimates that she can buy a large drink and a turkey sandwich, and still have enough money to get into the rink. Do you agree? Support your answer.

Sandwiches	Drinks
Tuna $3.95	Small $1.29
Turkey $4.85	Medium $1.59
Grilled Cheese $3.25	Large $1.79

_____

_____

_____

_____

_____

Number and Operations in Base Ten

1. Yolanda's sunflower plant was 64.34 centimeters tall in July. During August, the plant grew 58.7 centimeters. How tall was Yolanda's sunflower plant at the end of August?

   (A) 702.1 centimeters

   (B) 123.04 centimeters

   (C) 70.21 centimeters

   (D) 58.7 centimeters

2. Malcolm read that 2.75 inches of rain fell on Saturday. He read that 1.6 inches of rain fell on Sunday. How much rain fell on the two days?

   (A) 1.15 inches

   (B) 2.91 inches

   (C) 3.81 inches

   (D) 4.35 inches

3. Olivia bought a beach towel for $9.95 and a beach bag for $13.46. What is the total amount of money Olivia spent on the two items?

   (A) $12.31

   (B) $23.41

   (C) $112.96

   (D) $144.55

4. Jon walked 1.75 kilometers on Monday and 3.2 kilometers on Wednesday. What was the total distance that Jon walked on Monday and Wednesday?

   (A) 33.75 kilometers

   (B) 20.7 kilometers

   (C) 4.95 kilometers

   (D) 2.07 kilometers

5. Gavin and Miles hiked 3.45 kilometers on Tuesday morning. After lunch they hiked another 6.5 kilometers. Gavin says they hiked 9.5 kilometers in all. Describe Gavin's error and correct it.

   _____

   _____

   _____

   _____

   _____

   _____

   _____

1. Juan had a 10.75-pound block of clay. He used 4.6 pounds of clay to make a sculpture of a horse. How much clay does Juan have left?

   Ⓐ 6.1 pounds

   Ⓑ 6.15 pounds

   Ⓒ 10.29 pounds

   Ⓓ 15.35 pounds

2. Ella and Nick are meeting at the library. The library is 4.61 kilometers from Ella's house and 3.25 kilometers from Nick's house. How much farther does Ella live from the library than Nick?

   Ⓐ 1.36 kilometers

   Ⓑ 1.46 kilometers

   Ⓒ 7.86 kilometers

   Ⓓ 42.85 kilometers

3. Rafael bought 3.26 pounds of potato salad and 2.8 pounds of macaroni salad to bring to a picnic. How much more potato salad than macaroni salad did Rafael buy?

   Ⓐ 6.06 pounds

   Ⓑ 2.98 pounds

   Ⓒ 0.98 pound

   Ⓓ 0.46 pound

4. Salvador had 3.25 pounds of dry cement. He used 1.7 pounds to make a paver for his lawn. How many pounds of dry cement does Salvador have left?

   Ⓐ 1.55 pounds

   Ⓑ 2.08 pounds

   Ⓒ 3.08 pounds

   Ⓓ 4.95 pounds

5. The community center is 4.52 miles from Molly's house and 2.81 miles from Jacob's house. Explain how Molly might regroup in order to find out how much farther she lives from the community center than Jacob.

   _____

   _____

   _____

   _____

   _____

   _____

   _____

Number and Operations in Base Ten

1. Students are selling muffins at a school bake sale. One muffin costs $0.25, 2 muffins cost $0.37, 3 muffins cost $0.49, and 4 muffins cost $0.61. If this pattern continues, how much will 6 muffins cost?

   Ⓐ $0.73
   Ⓑ $0.83
   Ⓒ $0.85
   Ⓓ $0.97

2. Bob and Ling are playing a number sequence game. Bob wrote the following sequence.

   28.9, 26.8, 24.7, __?__, 20.5

   What is the unknown term in this sequence?

   Ⓐ 21.6
   Ⓑ 22.6
   Ⓒ 22.7
   Ⓓ 25.8

3. Students are selling handmade magnets at the school craft fair. One magnet costs $0.30, 2 magnets cost $0.43, 3 magnets cost $0.56, and 4 magnets cost $0.69. If this pattern continues, how much will 6 magnets cost?

   Ⓐ $0.82
   Ⓑ $0.93
   Ⓒ $0.95
   Ⓓ $1.02

4. Kevin and Yasuko are writing number sequences. Yasuko wrote the following number sequence.

   35.9, 34.7, 33.5, __?__, 31.1

   What is the unknown term in this sequence?

   Ⓐ 32.3
   Ⓑ 32.2
   Ⓒ 32
   Ⓓ 31.2

5. A beach resort rents snorkeling gear at $3.00 for 1 hour, $4.50 for 2 hours, $6.00 for 3 hours, and $7.50 for 4 hours. What rule could George use to find how much it will cost him to rent the gear for 6 hours? Explain how you found the rule.

   _____

   _____

   _____

   _____

Number and Operations in Base Ten

1. At the end of October, Mr. Diamond had a balance of $367.38 in his checking account. Since then, he has written two checks for $136.94 and $14.75 and made a deposit of $185.00. What is the balance in Mr. Diamond's checking account now?

   (A) $30.69
   (B) $334.07
   (C) $400.69
   (D) $704.07

2. Mario has $15. If he spends $6.25 on admission to the ice skating rink, $2.95 to rent skates, and $1.65 each for 2 hot chocolates, how much money will he have left?

   (A) $2.50
   (B) $3.50
   (C) $4.15
   (D) $10.85

3. Miguel has $20 to spend on going to a movie. If he spends $7.25 on a movie ticket, $3.95 for snacks, and $1.75 for bus fare each way, how much money will he have left?

   (A) $14.70
   (B) $7.05
   (C) $6.30
   (D) $5.30

4. At the end of November, Mrs. Gold had a balance of $426.83 in her checking account. Since then, she has written two checks for $163.49 and $16.85 and made a deposit of $195.00. What is the balance in Mrs. Gold's checking account now?

   (A) $51.49
   (B) $412.17
   (C) $441.49
   (D) $802.17

5. Each package of stickers that Olivia wants to buy costs $1.25. Olivia has $10. Explain how you can find the number of packages of stickers Olivia can buy.

   _____

   _____

   _____

   _____

   _____

Number and Operations in Base Ten

1. Della's cats weigh 9.8 and 8.25 pounds, and her dog weighs 25 pounds. How much more does her dog weigh than the total weight of both of her cats?

   (A)   6.95 pounds

   (B) 15.2 pounds

   (C) 16.75 pounds

   (D) 18.05 pounds

2. Rob used 4.25 ounces of peanuts, 3.4 ounces of pecans, and 2.75 ounces of walnuts to make a trail mix. How many ounces of nuts did Rob use in the trail mix?

   (A)   4.1 ounces

   (B)   4.865 ounces

   (C)   7.34 ounces

   (D) 10.4 ounces

3. Gina is training for a marathon. She ran 4.6 miles on Friday and 6.75 miles on Saturday. On Sunday, she ran 13 miles. How much farther did she run on Sunday than she did on Friday and Saturday combined?

   (A)   1.65 miles

   (B)   6.25 miles

   (C) 11.35 miles

   (D) 24.35 miles

4. Paul used 1.75 pounds of grapes, 2.6 pounds of bananas, and 3.25 pounds of apples to make fruit salad. How many pounds of fruit did Paul use in the salad?

   (A) 5.26 pounds

   (B) 6.6 pounds

   (C) 7.6 pounds

   (D) 8.6 pounds

5. William walked 2.75 miles on Friday, 3.6 miles on Saturday, and 4.25 miles on Sunday. Would you use mental math or place value to find how far William walked in all on the three days? Explain your choice.

   _____

   _____

   _____

   _____

   _____

1. Callie used a decimal model to help her multiply a decimal by a whole number. What equation does the model show?

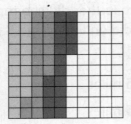

- (A) $3 \times 0.18 = 0.54$
- (B) $3 \times 0.18 = 5.4$
- (C) $18 \times 0.3 = 0.54$
- (D) $18 \times 0.3 = 5.4$

2. The weight of a dime is 0.08 ounce. Amad used a model to find the weight of 7 dimes. What is the weight of 7 dimes?

- (A) 0.54 ounce
- (C) 0.58 ounce
- (B) 0.56 ounce
- (D) 0.78 ounce

3. Miguel used a quick picture to help him multiply a decimal by a whole number. What equation does the model show?

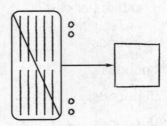

- (A) $2 \times 5.2 = 1.04$
- (B) $2 \times 5.2 = 10.4$
- (C) $2 \times 0.52 = 10.4$
- (D) $2 \times 0.52 = 1.04$

4. One serving of soup contains 0.45 gram of sodium. How much sodium is in 2 servings of the soup? You may use the decimal model to help you answer the question.

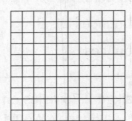

- (A) 0.09 gram
- (C) 9 grams
- (B) 0.9 gram
- (D) 90 grams

5. Ricardo walked to the library and back home. He lives 0.54 mile from the library. Draw a quick picture to find the distance Ricardo walked. Explain how you used the picture to solve the problem.

Number and Operations in Base Ten

1. Marci mailed 9 letters at the post office. Each letter weighed 3.5 ounces. What was the total weight of the letters that Marci mailed?

   (A) 33.5 ounces

   (B) 32.5 ounces

   (C) 31.5 ounces

   (D) 27.5 ounces

3. Mari and Rob are making a science poster. They need to write how much a rock that weighs 7 pounds on Earth would weigh on Mars. They know they can multiply weight on Earth by 0.38 to find weight on Mars. What number should they write on their poster?

   (A)   0.266 pound

   (B)   2.66 pounds

   (C)   26.6 pounds

   (D) 266 pounds

2. Laurie is in training for a race. When she trains, Laurie runs on a path that is 1.45 miles long. Last week, Laurie ran on this path 6 times. How many miles did Laurie run on the path last week?

   (A)   0.87 mile

   (B)   8.7 miles

   (C)   87 miles

   (D) 870 miles

4. Rhianna made a shelf to store her collection of rocks and shells. She used 5 pieces of wood that were each 3.25 feet long. How much wood did Rhianna use in all to make the shelf?

   (A)   6.25 feet

   (B) 15.05 feet

   (C) 15.25 feet

   (D) 16.25 feet

5. Arielle rode the Voyager roller coaster 4 times. A ride on the Voyager lasts 1.8 minutes. She rode the Cyclone roller coaster 3 times. A ride on the Cyclone lasts 2.45 minutes. Arielle says she spent more time on the Voyager than on the Cyclone. Do you agree? Support your answer.

   _____

   _____

   _____

   _____

   _____

Number and Operations in Base Ten

1. Ari is setting up a fish tank for his goldfish. The tank holds 15 gallons of water. The weight of a gallon of water rounded to the nearest tenth is 8.3 pounds. Ari used this weight to calculate the weight of the water in his fish tank. Which is the weight that Ari would find for the water in the fish tank?

   (A) 12.45 pounds
   (B) 16.5 pounds
   (C) 124.5 pounds
   (D) 165 pounds

2. Paul works at the local grocery store. He worked 15 hours this week. Last week, he worked 2.5 times as many hours as he worked this week. How many hours did Paul work last week?

   (A) 30.5 hours
   (B) 32.5 hours
   (C) 35 hours
   (D) 37.5 hours

3. The Barbers are keeping track of their family energy costs. It costs the Barbers $0.16 per week to run their dishwasher. How much will it cost them to run their dishwasher for 52 weeks?

   (A) $8.64
   (B) $8.32
   (C) $3.64
   (D) $1.92

4. Mrs. Green needs to store 21 math books on a shelf during school vacation. Each math book is 2.4 centimeters thick. If Mrs. Green stacks the math books on top of each other, how tall does the shelf have to be?

   (A) 12.6 centimeters
   (B) 40.4 centimeters
   (C) 50.4 centimeters
   (D) 54 centimeters

5. Sophia exchanged 1,000 U.S. dollars for the South African currency, which is called rand. The exchange rate was 7.15 rand to $1. How many South African rand did Sophia get? Explain how you know.

   _____

   _____

   _____

   _____

Number and Operations in Base Ten

1. At a dry cleaning store, it costs $1.79 to clean a man's dress shirt and $8.25 to clean a suit. Thomas brought in 4 shirts and 1 suit to be cleaned. How much will he be charged for the dry cleaning?

   (A) $15.41

   (B) $10.04

   (C) $8.95

   (D) $7.16

2. Mandy, Jeremy, and Lily went to an amusement park during their summer vacation. Mandy spent $16.25 at the amusement park. Jeremy spent $3.40 more than Mandy spent. Lily spent 2 times as much money as Jeremy spent. How much money did Lily spend at the amusement park?

   (A) $6.80   (C) $32.50

   (B) $19.65   (D) $39.30

3. Tim wants to rent a bike at the state park. It costs $3.95 per hour for the first 4 hours. After 4 hours, the cost is $2.50 per hour. How much would it cost Tim to rent a bike for 5 hours?

   (A) $19.75

   (B) $18.30

   (C) $15.80

   (D) $12.50

4. Peter spent $32.50 at the ballpark. Marty spent 5 times as much money as Peter spent. Callie spent $27.25 more than Marty. How much did Callie spend at the ballpark?

   (A) $59.75

   (B) $136.25

   (C) $162.50

   (D) $189.75

5. Chris collected $25.65 for a fundraiser. Remy collected $15.87 more than Chris did. Sandy collected 3 times as much as Remy. How much did Sandy collect for the fundraiser?
   Draw a diagram to solve. Then explain how you found your answer.

   _____

   _____

   _____

1. Keisha used this decimal model to help her multiply. What equation does the model show?

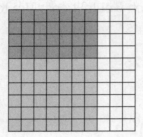

(A) $4 \times 7 = 28$ (C) $0.4 \times 0.7 = 0.28$

(B) $4 \times 0.7 = 2.8$ (D) $0.4 \times 7 = 2.8$

2. Lorenzo had a piece of wire that was 0.6 meter long. He used 0.5 of the wire. How much wire did Lorenzo use?

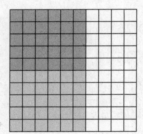

(A) 0.03 meter   (C) 0.3 meter

(B) 0.1 meter   (D) 1.1 meters

3. Mickey used a decimal model to help him multiply 0.3×0.8. What is the product of 0.3 and 0.8?

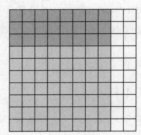

(A) 0.024   (C) 2.4

(B) 0.24   (D) 24

4. One serving of a dried fruit mix contains 0.9 gram of potassium. How much potassium is in 0.5 serving of the dried fruit mix? You may use the decimal model to help you answer the question.

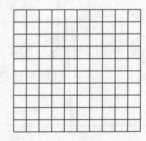

(A) 0.45 gram   (C) 4.5 grams

(B) 1.4 grams   (D) 45 grams

5. Arina bought 0.9 yard of material. She used 0.8 of the material to make place mats. Use the decimal model to show how much material she used. Then explain how you found the answer.

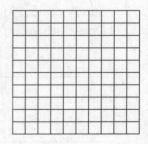

_____

_____

_____

_____

Number and Operations in Base Ten

1. A scientist at a giant panda preserve in China measured the length of a newborn cub as 15.5 centimeters. The cub's mother was 9.5 times as tall as the length of the cub. How tall is the mother?

Ⓐ   14.725 centimeters

Ⓑ   25 centimeters

Ⓒ 147.25 centimeters

Ⓓ 1,472.5 centimeters

2. Emily stopped at a produce stand to buy some tomatoes. Tomatoes cost $1.25 per pound at the stand. Emily bought 5 tomatoes that weighed a total of 1.8 pounds. How much did Emily pay for the tomatoes?

Ⓐ $2.25

Ⓑ $3.05

Ⓒ $6.25

Ⓓ $22.50

3. Mel's father asked Mel to mow his lawn while he was on vacation. Mel bought 1.6 gallons of gas for the lawn mower. The gas cost $2.85 per gallon. How much money did Mel pay for the gas?

Ⓐ $45.60

Ⓑ $4.56

Ⓒ $4.45

Ⓓ $4.13

4. Mr. Harris has 54.8 acres of land. Mr. Fitz has 0.35 times as many acres as Mr. Harris has. How many acres of land does Mr. Fitz have?

Ⓐ 4.384 acres

Ⓑ 19.108 acres

Ⓒ 19.18 acres

Ⓓ 43.84 acres

5. Mr. Evans is paid $9.20 per hour for the first 40 hours he works in a week. He is paid 1.5 times that rate for each hour he works after that. Last week Mr. Evans worked 42.25 hours. He says he earned more than $400 last week. Do you agree? Support your answer.

_____

_____

_____

_____

_____

Number and Operations in Base Ten

1. Denise, Keith, and Tim live in the same neighborhood. Denise lives 0.3 mile from Keith. The distance that Tim and Keith live from each other is 0.2 times longer than the distance between Denise and Keith. How far from each other do Tim and Keith live?

   (A) 0.6 mile

   (B) 0.5 mile

   (C) 0.1 mile

   (D) 0.06 mile

2. Tina is making a special dessert for her brother's birthday. Tina's recipe calls for 0.5 kilogram of flour. The recipe also calls for an amount of sugar that is 0.8 times as much as the amount of flour. How much sugar will Tina need to make the dessert?

   (A) 4 kilograms

   (B) 0.4 kilogram

   (C) 0.04 kilogram

   (D) 0.004 kilogram

3. The information booklet for a video console says that the console uses about 0.2 kilowatt of electricity per hour. If electricity costs $0.15 per kilowatt hour, how much does it cost to run the console for an hour?

   (A) $0.03

   (B) $0.30

   (C) $3.00

   (D) $30.00

4. Bruce is getting materials for a chemistry experiment. His teacher gives him a container that holds 0.25 liter of a blue liquid. Bruce needs to use 0.4 of this liquid for the experiment. How much blue liquid will Bruce use?

   (A) 0.001 liter

   (B) 0.01 liter

   (C) 0.1 liter

   (D) 1 liter

5. Ashton bought a new laptop computer that uses about 0.4 kilowatt of electricity per hour. Electricity costs $0.10 per kilowatt hour. Explain how you can find how much it costs to use the laptop for one hour.

   _____

   _____

   _____

   _____

1. Emilio used a model to help him divide 2.46 by 2. What is the quotient?

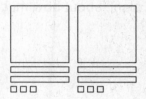

Ⓐ 1.23
Ⓑ 1.32
Ⓒ 3.21
Ⓓ 12.3

2. Heath bought 1.2 pounds of potato salad. He divided it into 4 containers, each with the same amount. How much potato salad was in each container?

Ⓐ 0.03 pound
Ⓑ 0.3 pound
Ⓒ 0.8 pound
Ⓓ 4.8 pounds

3. Theo made a model to represent a division statement. What division statement does the model show?

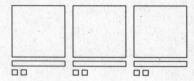

Ⓐ 3.12 ÷ 3 = 1.12
Ⓑ 3.63 ÷ 3 = 1.21
Ⓒ 2.24 ÷ 2 = 1.12
Ⓓ 3.36 ÷ 3 = 1.12

4. Maya practiced the piano for 3.75 hours last week. If she practiced the same amount of time each of 5 days, how long did she practice each day?

Ⓐ 0.25 hour
Ⓑ 0.5 hour
Ⓒ 0.75 hour
Ⓓ 1.25 hours

5. Nina bought 3.24 pounds of ground beef and made 3 packages from it. Each package had the same amount of ground beef. How can you use base-ten blocks to model how much ground beef Nina put in each package?

_____

_____

_____

_____

_____

_____

1. Ashleigh rode her bicycle 26.5 miles in 4 hours. Which gives the **best** estimate of how far Ashleigh rode in 1 hour?

   (A) 0.5 mile

   (B) 0.6 mile

   (C) 5 miles

   (D) 7 miles

2. Ellen drove 357.9 miles. Her car gets about 21 miles per gallon. Which is the **best** estimate of how many gallons of gas Ellen used?

   (A) 17 gallons

   (B) 16 gallons

   (C) 1.7 gallons

   (D) 0.17 gallon

3. Landon bought a box of plants for $8.79. There were 16 plants in the box. If Landon had bought only 1 plant, about how much would it have cost?

   (A) about $0.40

   (B) about $0.50

   (C) about $0.60

   (D) about $0.70

4. Josh bought a 34.6-pound bag of dry dog food to feed his dogs. The bag lasted 8 days. About how much dog food did his dogs eat each day?

   (A) about 0.4 pound

   (B) about 0.5 pound

   (C) about 4 pounds

   (D) about 5 pounds

5. Karl drove 624.3 miles. He used a total of 31 gallons of gas in his car. How can Karl estimate how many miles per gallon his car gets?

   _____

   _____

   _____

   _____

   _____

1. Grant is making small bags of dried fruit from a large bag of dried fruit that weighs 5.46 pounds. If he puts the same amount of dried fruit in each of 6 bags, how much will each bag weigh?

   (A) 0.0091 pound

   (B) 0.091 pound

   (C) 0.91 pound

   (D) 9.1 pounds

2. Mia has a piece of ribbon that is 30.5 yards long. The length is just enough ribbon to make 5 bows that are the same size. How long is the ribbon that she uses for each bow?

   (A) 6.01 yards

   (B) 6.1 yards

   (C) 6.2 yards

   (D) 6.5 yards

3. A plumber has a piece of copper tubing that is 112.8 inches long. He needs to cut the tubing into 12 equal pieces to repair some leaky pipes. How long will each piece of tubing be?

   (A) 0.094 inch

   (B) 0.94 inch

   (C) 9.4 inches

   (D) 94 inches

4. Matthew bought 13 used video games that were on sale in a store. He paid $84.37 for the games. If each video game cost the same price, how much did 1 video game cost?

   (A) $6.09

   (B) $6.19

   (C) $6.39

   (D) $6.49

5. Chase can buy a pack of baseball cards that contains 24 cards for $3.84, or he can buy a pack that contains 60 cards for $8.40. Chase wants to buy the pack of baseball cards that is the better buy. Which pack should he buy? Support your answer.

   _____

   _____

   _____

   _____

   _____

1. Peter used a model to help him divide 0.28 by 0.07. What is the quotient?

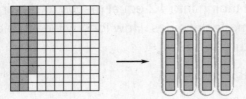

   (A) 0.04

   (B) 0.4

   (C) 4

   (D) 28

2. Heather used 1.5 pounds of roast beef. She used it all in sandwiches. She used 0.5 pound in each sandwich. How many sandwiches did she make?

   (A) 0.3

   (B) 3

   (C) 4.5

   (D) 30

3. Fiona made the model below to represent a division statement. What division statement does the model show?

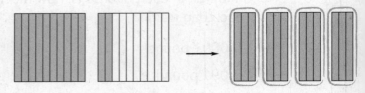

   (A) $1.2 \div 0.3 = 4$

   (B) $1.2 \div 0.4 = 3$

   (C) $1.6 \div 0.4 = 4$

   (D) $0.9 \div 0.3 = 3$

4. Tyrone used 3.75 cups of hot water to make hot chocolate. He poured 0.75 cup of hot water into each mug of chocolate. How many mugs of hot chocolate did he make?

   (A) 3

   (B) 4

   (C) 5

   (D) 6

5. Eddie paid $0.80 for some pencils. Each pencil cost $0.16. Explain how to use a model to find how many pencils Eddie bought.

   _____

   _____

   _____

   _____

   _____

1. Leilani bought tomatoes that cost $0.84 per pound. She paid $3.36 for the tomatoes. How many pounds of tomatoes did she buy?

   (A) 0.004 pound

   (B) 0.04 pound

   (C) 0.4 pound

   (D) 4 pounds

2. Carly has a piece of yarn that is 7.2 yards long. She needs to cut the yarn into pieces of fringe that each measure 0.3 yard long. How many pieces of fringe can she cut from the piece of yarn?

   (A) 2,400

   (B) 240

   (C) 24

   (D) 2.4

3. Latisha hiked along a trail that was 9.66 miles long last Saturday. It took her 4.2 hours to complete the trail. What was Latisha's average speed per hour?

   (A) 0.23 mile per hour

   (B) 2.3 miles per hour

   (C) 20.3 miles per hour

   (D) 23 miles per hour

4. Quan records that his hamster can turn the wheel in its cage to make 1 revolution in 0.5 minute. How many revolutions can the hamster make in 20.5 minutes?

   (A) 4.1

   (B) 41

   (C) 410

   (D) 4,100

5. Shareen walked a total of 9.52 miles in a walk-a-thon. She completed the walk in 3.4 hours. She wanted to find her average walking speed. Explain why Shareen might begin by multiplying 3.4 and 9.52 by the same power of ten to solve the problem.

   _____

   _____

   _____

   _____

   _____

1. Tony collected 16.2 pounds of pecans from the trees at his farm. He will give the same weight of pecans to each of 12 friends. How many pounds of pecans will each friend get?

   (A)   0.135 pound

   (B)   1.35 pounds

   (C)   13.5 pounds

   (D)   135 pounds

2. Trevor drove 202 miles to visit his grandparents. It took him 4 hours to get there. What was the average speed that Trevor drove?

   (A)   5.05 miles per hour

   (B)   5.5 miles per hour

   (C)   50.5 miles per hour

   (D)   55 miles per hour

3. Denise's mother bought some zucchini for $0.78 per pound. If she paid $2.73 for the zucchini, how many pounds of zucchini did she buy?

   (A)   0.35 pound

   (B)   3.5 pounds

   (C)   35 pounds

   (D)   350 pounds

4. The students at Winwood Elementary School collected 574 cans of food in 20 days for a food drive. What was the average number of cans of food collected each day?

   (A)   2.87

   (B)   27

   (C)   28

   (D) 28.7

5. Cynthia bought some grapes on sale for $0.94 per pound. She paid $2.35 for the grapes. Cynthia said that she bought between 2 and 3 pounds of grapes. Do you agree with Cynthia? Support your answer.

   _____

   _____

   _____

   _____

   _____

   _____

Number and Operations in Base Ten

1. Reshawn is buying 3 books in a set for $24.81. He will save $6.69 by buying the set instead of buying individual books. If each book costs the same amount, how much does each of the 3 books cost when purchased individually?

   Ⓐ $2.23

   Ⓑ $6.04

   Ⓒ $8.27

   Ⓓ $10.50

2. Mackenzie spent a total of $17.50 on Saturday afternoon. She bought a movie ticket for $7.25 and snacks for $4.95. She spent the rest of the money on bus fare to get to the movie and back home. How much was the bus fare each way if each trip cost the same amount?

   Ⓐ $2.60   Ⓒ $5.20

   Ⓑ $2.65   Ⓓ $5.30

3. Corey and Nicole spent $17.00, including sales tax, on 2 sandwiches and 3 slices of pizza. The sandwiches cost $5.25 each and the total sales tax was $0.92. How much did each slice of pizza cost?

   Ⓐ $1.86

   Ⓑ $2.47

   Ⓒ $2.79

   Ⓓ $5.58

4. Jocelyn bought 2 sweaters for the same price. She paid $23.56, including sales tax of $1.36 and a $5.00 coupon. What was the price of one sweater before the tax and coupon?

   Ⓐ $8.60

   Ⓑ $19.96

   Ⓒ $13.60

   Ⓓ $14.96

5. Samantha bought flowers at a craft store for $14.02. She also bought 4 packages of glass beads and 2 vases. The vases cost $3.59 each and the total sales tax was $1.34. The total amount she paid was $28.50, including sales tax. Explain a strategy you would use to find the cost of one package of glass beads.

   _____

   _____

   _____

   _____

   _____

   _____

Number and Operations in Base Ten

1. Arturo wants to find the amount of time he spent on his math and science homework combined. He worked $\frac{2}{5}$ hour on math and $\frac{1}{3}$ hour on science. Which is the **best** strategy to find the least common denominator so he can add the time he spent on his homework?

   (A) Multiply denominators since they share no common factors other than 1.

   (B) Find all the multiples of each denominator.

   (C) One denominator is the multiple of the other, so the multiple is the least common denominator.

   (D) Add the denominators to find the least common multiple.

2. Francine wants to find the total of $\frac{2}{3}$ cup of blueberries and $\frac{5}{8}$ cup of raspberries. What is the least common denominator of the fractions?

   (A) 10   (C) 18

   (B) 11   (D) 24

3. Alana bought $\frac{3}{8}$ pound of Swiss cheese and $\frac{1}{4}$ pound of American cheese. Which pair of fractions **cannot** be used to find how many pounds of cheese she bought in all?

   (A) $\frac{6}{16}$ and $\frac{4}{16}$

   (B) $\frac{9}{24}$ and $\frac{6}{24}$

   (C) $\frac{24}{64}$ and $\frac{8}{64}$

   (D) $\frac{15}{40}$ and $\frac{10}{40}$

4. Charles bought $\frac{7}{8}$ foot of electrical wire and $\frac{5}{6}$ foot of copper wire for his science project. What is the least common denominator of the fractions?

   (A) 14

   (B) 18

   (C) 24

   (D) 48

5. On Saturday, Percy biked for $6\frac{3}{12}$ hours. On Sunday, he biked for $5\frac{2}{3}$ hours. Explain how to find the least common denominator of these two fractions.

_____

_____

_____

_____

Number and Operations–Fractions

1. Brady used $\frac{2}{3}$ gallon of yellow paint and $\frac{1}{4}$ gallon of white paint to paint his dresser. How many gallons of paint did Brady use?

   Ⓐ $\frac{3}{7}$ gallon

   Ⓑ $\frac{3}{4}$ gallon

   Ⓒ $\frac{5}{6}$ gallon

   Ⓓ $\frac{11}{12}$ gallon

2. Mr. Barber uses $\frac{7}{9}$ yard of wire to put up a ceiling fan. He uses $\frac{1}{3}$ yard of wire to fix a switch. How much more wire does he use to put up the fan than to fix the switch?

   Ⓐ $1\frac{1}{9}$ yards

   Ⓑ $\frac{6}{9}$ yard

   Ⓒ $\frac{4}{9}$ yard

   Ⓓ $\frac{1}{3}$ yard

3. Tom jogged $\frac{3}{5}$ mile on Monday and $\frac{2}{6}$ mile on Tuesday. How much farther did Tom jog on Monday than on Tuesday?

   Ⓐ $\frac{1}{30}$ mile

   Ⓑ $\frac{3}{15}$ mile

   Ⓒ $\frac{8}{30}$ mile

   Ⓓ $\frac{14}{15}$ mile

4. Mindy bought $\frac{1}{6}$ pound of almonds and $\frac{3}{4}$ pound of walnuts. How many pounds of nuts did she buy in all?

   Ⓐ $\frac{1}{3}$

   Ⓑ $\frac{7}{12}$

   Ⓒ $\frac{2}{3}$

   Ⓓ $\frac{11}{12}$

5. George worked on his science project for $\frac{5}{12}$ hour on Monday and $\frac{3}{4}$ hour on Tuesday. How much longer did George work on his science project on Tuesday than on Monday? Explain how you found your answer.

_____

_____

_____

Number and Operations–Fractions

1. David practices piano for $1\frac{1}{3}$ hours on Monday and $3\frac{1}{2}$ hours on Tuesday. How much longer does he practice piano on Tuesday than on Monday?

Ⓐ $1\frac{1}{5}$ hours

Ⓑ $2\frac{1}{6}$ hours

Ⓒ $2\frac{2}{5}$ hours

Ⓓ $2\frac{5}{6}$ hours

2. Roberto's cat weighed $6\frac{3}{4}$ pounds last year. The cat weighs $1\frac{1}{2}$ pounds more now. How much does the cat weigh now?

Ⓐ $5\frac{1}{4}$ pounds

Ⓑ $7\frac{1}{4}$ pounds

Ⓒ $7\frac{3}{4}$ pounds

Ⓓ $8\frac{1}{4}$ pounds

3. Ken bought $3\frac{3}{4}$ pounds of apples at the farmers' market. Abby bought $2\frac{1}{8}$ pounds of apples. How many pounds of apples did Ken and Abby buy in all?

Ⓐ $5\frac{1}{8}$ pounds   Ⓒ $5\frac{7}{8}$ pounds

Ⓑ $5\frac{1}{3}$ pounds   Ⓓ $6\frac{1}{4}$ pounds

4. Three students made videos for their art project. The table shows the length of each video.

Art in Nature

Video	Length (in hours)
1	$4\frac{3}{4}$
2	$2\frac{7}{12}$
3	$2\frac{1}{6}$

How much longer is video 1 than video 3?

Ⓐ $1\frac{5}{12}$ hours   Ⓒ $2\frac{5}{12}$ hours

Ⓑ $1\frac{7}{12}$ hours   Ⓓ $2\frac{7}{12}$ hours

5. It takes Evan $6\frac{3}{4}$ hours to mow 3 lawns. It takes him $2\frac{1}{3}$ hours to mow Mr. Garcia's lawn and $1\frac{3}{4}$ hours to mow Miss Pasteur's lawn. How many hours does it take Evan to mow the third lawn? Explain how you found your answer.

_____

_____

_____

_____

_____

_____

1. Kyle is hanging wallpaper in his bedroom. A roll of wallpaper is $18\frac{3}{8}$ feet long. Kyle cut off a piece of wallpaper $2\frac{5}{6}$ feet long. How much wallpaper is left on the roll?

   (A) $15\frac{13}{24}$ feet

   (B) $15\frac{7}{12}$ feet

   (C) $16\frac{13}{24}$ feet

   (D) $17\frac{3}{8}$ feet

2. Giselle made $24\frac{1}{8}$ ounces of lemonade. She sampled $1\frac{1}{2}$ ounces to make sure it is not too sour. How much lemonade is left?

   (A) $23\frac{9}{8}$ ounces

   (B) $23\frac{5}{8}$ ounces

   (C) $22\frac{5}{8}$ ounces

   (D) $22\frac{5}{16}$ ounces

3. Maria needs a piece of string $4\frac{2}{3}$ feet long for a science project. She cuts it from a piece that is $7\frac{1}{12}$ feet long. How much string does she have left?

   (A) $11\frac{3}{4}$ feet

   (B) $3\frac{5}{12}$ feet

   (C) $2\frac{7}{12}$ feet

   (D) $2\frac{5}{12}$ feet

4. Taylor saw an American alligator at a zoo that measured $12\frac{11}{12}$ feet long. The record length of an American alligator is $19\frac{1}{6}$ feet long. How much longer is the record alligator than the alligator Taylor saw?

   (A) $5\frac{5}{8}$ feet

   (B) $5\frac{7}{8}$ feet

   (C) $6\frac{1}{4}$ feet

   (D) $6\frac{1}{3}$ feet

5. Mr. Carlson has $1\frac{3}{8}$ acres of land. His house and yard cover $\frac{7}{8}$ acre and he uses the rest of his land to grow corn. Mr. Carlson states that he uses most of his land to grow corn. Describe Mr. Carlson's statement as true or false, and explain why.

   _____

   _____

   _____

   _____

1. Carrie is given a plant. After one week, it grows to $\frac{7}{8}$ foot tall, and after two weeks it grows to $1\frac{1}{2}$ feet tall. If it keeps growing at the same pace, how tall will it be after 3 weeks?

   (A) $2\frac{1}{4}$ feet

   (B) $2\frac{1}{8}$ feet

   (C) $1\frac{7}{8}$ feet

   (D) $1\frac{5}{8}$ feet

2. Chan ran a race course in $1\frac{3}{5}$ hours. The following month, he ran the same course in $1\frac{3}{10}$ hours. If his time improves by the same amount each month, how long will it take to run the course after another month?

   (A) $\frac{4}{5}$ hour

   (B) $\frac{9}{10}$ hour

   (C) 1 hour

   (D) $1\frac{1}{5}$ hours

3. When Bruce started bowling, he won $\frac{1}{4}$ of the games he played. Within six months, he was winning $\frac{7}{16}$ of his games. If he improves at the same rate, what fraction of his games should he expect to win after another six months?

   (A) $\frac{1}{2}$

   (B) $\frac{9}{16}$

   (C) $\frac{5}{8}$

   (D) $\frac{11}{16}$

4. A farm produced $1\frac{1}{8}$ tons of corn in its first year, $1\frac{3}{8}$ tons in its second year, and $1\frac{10}{16}$ tons in its third year. If the pattern continues each year, how much corn did the farm produce in the fourth year?

   (A) $1\frac{12}{16}$ tons

   (B) $1\frac{7}{8}$ tons

   (C) $1\frac{3}{4}$ tons

   (D) $1\frac{5}{16}$ tons

5. When Jill started jogging, she ran $\frac{3}{4}$ mile on the first day, $1\frac{1}{8}$ miles on the second day, and $1\frac{1}{2}$ miles on the third day. If she increases the distance she jogs each day by the same amount, how far will she jog on the fifth day? Explain how you found your answer.

   _____

   _____

   _____

   _____

   _____

Number and Operations–Fractions

1. Ava hiked a trail that has three sections that are $4\frac{7}{8}$ miles, $3\frac{3}{4}$ miles, and $5\frac{1}{8}$ miles long. Ava wrote this expression to show the total distance that she hiked.

$$\left(4\frac{7}{8} + 3\frac{3}{4}\right) + 5\frac{1}{8}$$

Which shows another way to write the expression using only the Commutative Property of Addition?

Ⓐ $4\frac{7}{8} + \left(3\frac{3}{4} + 5\frac{1}{8}\right)$
Ⓑ $\left(5\frac{1}{8} + 4\frac{7}{8}\right) + 3\frac{3}{4}$
Ⓒ $\left(3\frac{3}{4} + 4\frac{7}{8}\right) + 5\frac{1}{8}$
Ⓓ $(4 + 3 + 5) + \left(\frac{7}{8} + \frac{3}{4} + \frac{1}{8}\right)$

2. Shelley wove three rugs with geometric designs. She wrote this expression to show the total length in feet of all three rugs.

$$\left(8\frac{7}{16} + 11\frac{7}{8}\right) + 15\frac{1}{4}$$

Which shows another way to write the expression using the Associative Property of Addition?

Ⓐ $8\frac{7}{16} + \left(15\frac{7}{8} + 11\frac{1}{4}\right)$
Ⓑ $8\frac{7}{16} + \left(11\frac{7}{8} + 15\frac{1}{4}\right)$
Ⓒ $\left(8\frac{7}{16} + 11\frac{7}{8}\right) + \left(8\frac{7}{16} + 15\frac{1}{4}\right)$
Ⓓ $(8 + 11 + 15) + \left(\frac{7}{16} + \frac{7}{8} + \frac{1}{4}\right)$

3. Larry wrote this expression to show the total number of hours he spent driving during the last three weeks.

$$\left(5\frac{2}{5} + 7\frac{4}{10}\right) + 9\frac{1}{10}$$

Which shows another way to write the expression using the Associative Property of Addition?

Ⓐ $5\frac{2}{5} + \left(7\frac{4}{10} + 9\frac{1}{10}\right)$
Ⓑ $5\frac{2}{5} + \left(9\frac{1}{10} + 7\frac{4}{10}\right)$
Ⓒ $\left(7\frac{4}{10} + 9\frac{1}{10}\right) + 5\frac{2}{5}$
Ⓓ $(5 + 9 + 4) + \left(\frac{2}{5} + \frac{4}{10} + \frac{1}{10}\right)$

4. Marco wrote the following expression to find the total amount of gasoline he bought last month.

$$8\frac{1}{5} + 6\frac{1}{8} + 7\frac{3}{5}$$

Which expression will help make the addition easier for Marco?

Ⓐ $\left(8\frac{1}{5} + 6\frac{1}{8}\right) + 7\frac{3}{5}$
Ⓑ $\left(7\frac{3}{5} + 6\frac{1}{8}\right) + 8\frac{1}{5}$
Ⓒ $\left(8\frac{1}{5} + 7\frac{3}{5}\right) + 6\frac{1}{8}$
Ⓓ $\left(8\frac{1}{5} + 7\frac{3}{5}\right) + 6\frac{1}{5}$

5. Stephen has three fish tanks that hold $5\frac{2}{3}$ gallons, $3\frac{5}{8}$ gallons, and $4\frac{1}{3}$ gallons. He wants to put the water from the three tanks into one new tank. Explain the easiest way for him to find the minimum size the new tank should be.

_____

_____

_____

Use the information for 1-2.

Addison used $\frac{5}{6}$ yard of ribbon to decorate a photo frame. She used $\frac{1}{3}$ yard of ribbon to decorate her scrapbook.

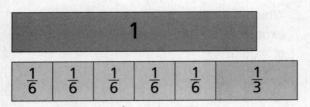

1. Which fraction strips should Addison trade for the $\frac{1}{3}$ strip in order to find how many yards of ribbon she used in all?

   (A) $\frac{1}{2}$ (C) $\frac{1}{4}$

   (B) $\frac{1}{3}$ (D) $\frac{1}{6}$

2. How many yards of ribbon did Addison use in all?

   (A) $1\frac{1}{6}$ yards   (C) $\frac{5}{9}$ yard

   (B) 1 yard   (D) $\frac{1}{2}$ yard

Use the information for 3-4.

Gabrielle paints a flower pot to sell at the craft fair. She paints $\frac{2}{5}$ of the pot teal, $\frac{3}{10}$ of the pot yellow, and the rest of the pot white.

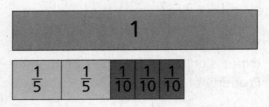

3. Which fraction strips should Gabrielle trade for the $\frac{2}{5}$ strip in order to find how much of the pot is painted teal or yellow?

   (A) $\frac{1}{2}$ (C) $\frac{1}{10}$

   (B) $\frac{1}{5}$ (D) $\frac{1}{15}$

4. How much of the pot is painted teal or yellow?

   (A) $\frac{1}{10}$ (C) $\frac{1}{2}$

   (B) $\frac{5}{15}$ (D) $\frac{7}{10}$

5. Juan needs $\frac{1}{4}$ cup of flour to make muffins and $\frac{3}{8}$ cup to make brownies. Draw fraction strips to help you find the total amount of flour Juan needs. Explain your work.

_____

_____

_____

Number and Operations–Fractions

Use the information for 1-2.

Armand lives $\frac{7}{8}$ mile from school. On his way home from school, he rode his skateboard $\frac{5}{16}$ mile and walked the rest of the way.

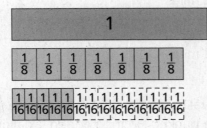

1. How many $\frac{1}{16}$ fraction strips are equal to $\frac{7}{8}$?

    (A) 5

    (B) 7

    (C) 8

    (D) 14

2. How far did Armand walk?

    (A) $\frac{1}{8}$ mile

    (B) $\frac{1}{2}$ mile

    (C) $\frac{9}{16}$ mile

    (D) $1\frac{1}{8}$ miles

Use the information for 3-4.

Kim has a piece of cardboard that is $\frac{5}{6}$ inch long. She cut off a $\frac{5}{12}$-inch piece.

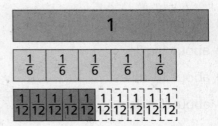

3. How many $\frac{1}{12}$ fraction strips are equal to $\frac{5}{6}$?

    (A) 5

    (B) 6

    (C) 10

    (D) 12

4. How long is the remaining piece of cardboard?

    (A) $\frac{10}{12}$ inch

    (B) $\frac{5}{12}$ inch

    (C) $\frac{1}{3}$ inch

    (D) $\frac{1}{6}$ inch

5. Ami spent $\frac{5}{6}$ hour doing math and science homework, with $\frac{1}{4}$ hour spent on math. Draw fraction strips to help you find how much time Ami spent on science homework. Explain your work.

    _____

    _____

    _____

1. Ron walked $\frac{8}{10}$ mile from his grandmother's house to the store. Then he walked $\frac{9}{10}$ mile to his house. About how far did he walk altogether?

   (A) about $\frac{1}{2}$ mile

   (B) about 1 mile

   (C) about $1\frac{1}{2}$ miles

   (D) about 2 miles

2. Sophia baby-sat for $3\frac{7}{12}$ hours on Friday. She baby-sat $2\frac{5}{6}$ hours on Saturday. Which is the **best** estimate of how many hours Sophia baby-sat altogether?

   (A) about $5\frac{1}{2}$ hours

   (B) about 6 hours

   (C) about $6\frac{1}{2}$ hours

   (D) about 7 hours

3. Three fences on a ranch measure $\frac{15}{16}$ mile, $\frac{7}{8}$ mile, and $\frac{7}{16}$ mile. Which is the **best** estimate of the total length of all three fences?

   (A) $1\frac{1}{2}$ miles

   (B) 2 miles

   (C) $2\frac{1}{2}$ miles

   (D) 3 miles

4. Mr. Krasa poured $\frac{5}{16}$ gallon of white paint into a bucket. He then added $\frac{3}{4}$ gallon of blue paint and $\frac{3}{8}$ gallon of red paint. Which is the **best** estimate of the total amount of paint in the bucket?

   (A) $\frac{3}{4}$ gallon

   (B) 1 gallon

   (C) $1\frac{1}{2}$ gallons

   (D) 3 gallons

5. Gina wants to ship three books that weigh $2\frac{7}{16}$ pounds, $1\frac{7}{8}$ pounds and $\frac{1}{2}$ pound. The maximum weight she can ship is 5 pounds. Estimate to see if Gina can ship all 3 books. Explain your answer.

_____

_____

_____

_____

_____

_____

_____

1. Jacques caught 3 fish weighing a total of $23\frac{1}{2}$ pounds. Two of the fish weighed $9\frac{5}{8}$ and $6\frac{1}{4}$ pounds. How much did the third fish weigh?

   (A) $6\frac{5}{8}$ pounds

   (B) $7\frac{3}{8}$ pounds

   (C) $7\frac{5}{8}$ pounds

   (D) $8\frac{3}{8}$ pounds

2. Maria bought a total of $1\frac{3}{4}$ dozen bagels. Of the total, she bought $\frac{1}{6}$ dozen whole grain bagels, $\frac{3}{4}$ dozen sesame seed bagels, and some plain bagels. How many dozen plain bagels did Maria buy?

   (A) $\frac{5}{6}$ dozen

   (B) 1 dozen

   (C) $\frac{11}{12}$ dozen

   (D) $2\frac{2}{3}$ dozen

3. A squash, an apple, and an orange weigh a total of $2\frac{3}{8}$ pounds. The squash weighs $1\frac{15}{16}$ pounds, and the apple weighs $\frac{1}{4}$ pound. How much does the orange weigh?

   (A) $\frac{1}{8}$ pound

   (B) $\frac{3}{16}$ pound

   (C) $\frac{1}{4}$ pound

   (D) $\frac{5}{16}$ pound

4. Kelsey entered the triathlon at Camp Meadowlark. The total distance was $15\frac{11}{16}$ miles. The bike segment was $12\frac{1}{4}$ miles, and the running segment was $3\frac{1}{16}$ miles. How long was the swimming segment?

   (A) $\frac{3}{16}$ mile

   (B) $\frac{1}{4}$ mile

   (C) $\frac{5}{16}$ mile

   (D) $\frac{3}{8}$ mile

5. In three days this week, Julio worked $18\frac{7}{10}$ total hours. He worked $6\frac{1}{5}$ hours on the first day and $6\frac{2}{5}$ hours on the second day. Explain how you would find the number of hours Julio worked on the third day.

_____

_____

_____

_____

_____

_____

_____

_____

Number and Operations–Fractions

1. Taylor took 560 photographs during summer vacation. She placed 12 photos on each page of her scrapbook, except the last page. She had fewer than 12 photos to put on the last page. How many photos did Taylor place on the last page of the scrapbook?

   (A) 7   (C) 9

   (B) 8   (D) 10

2. Marla filled up her car's gas tank and then went on a trip. After she drove 329 miles, she filled her tank with 14 gallons of gas. If she drove the same number of miles on each gallon of gas, how many miles per gallon did Marla drive?

   (A) 23 miles per gallon

   (B) $23\frac{1}{2}$ miles per gallon

   (C) 24 miles per gallon

   (D) $24\frac{1}{2}$ miles per gallon

3. Kate made 180 ounces of punch for a party. She pours 8 ounces of punch for one serving. How many people can have a full serving?

   (A) 22

   (B) $22\frac{1}{2}$

   (C) 23

   (D) 25

4. The pool director has a list of 123 students who have signed up for swimming lessons. The pool director can register 7 students in each class. What is the **least** number of classes needed for all the students to be registered in a class?

   (A) 16   (C) 18

   (B) 17   (D) 19

5. Molly has a weekend job picking apples. She picked 1,078 apples last weekend and put them in bags that hold 12 apples each. How many bags containing exactly 12 apples each did Molly fill? Explain how you used the quotient and the remainder to answer the question.

   _____

   _____

   _____

   _____

© Houghton Mifflin Harcourt Publishing Company

Number and Operations–Fractions

1. Four friends share 3 apples equally. What fraction of an apple does each friend get?

   Ⓐ $\frac{2}{3}$

   Ⓑ $\frac{3}{4}$

   Ⓒ $1\frac{1}{4}$

   Ⓓ $1\frac{1}{3}$

2. Ten pounds of rice are distributed equally into 6 bags to give out at the food bank. How many pounds of rice are in each bag?

   Ⓐ $\frac{3}{5}$ pound

   Ⓑ $1\frac{1}{3}$ pounds

   Ⓒ $1\frac{2}{3}$ pounds

   Ⓓ $1\frac{4}{5}$ pounds

3. Twelve friends share 4 pizzas equally. What fraction of a pizza does each friend get?

   Ⓐ $\frac{1}{12}$

   Ⓑ $\frac{1}{3}$

   Ⓒ $\frac{1}{4}$

   Ⓓ $\frac{1}{2}$

4. Terry picked 7 pounds of strawberries. She wants to share the strawberries equally among 3 of her neighbors. How many pounds of strawberries will each neighbor get?

   Ⓐ $\frac{3}{7}$ pound

   Ⓑ $\frac{7}{10}$ pound

   Ⓒ $1\frac{3}{7}$ pounds

   Ⓓ $2\frac{1}{3}$ pounds

5. Jake baked 5 cherry pies. He wants to share them equally among 3 of his neighbors. Jake says that each neighbor will get $\frac{3}{5}$ of a cherry pie. Do you agree? Support your answer.

   _____

   _____

   _____

   _____

1. Sophie uses 18 beads to make a necklace. Three-sixths of the beads are purple. How many of Sophie's beads are purple?

   Ⓐ 6
   Ⓑ 9
   Ⓒ 12
   Ⓓ 15

2. Charlotte bought 16 songs. Three-fourths of the songs are pop songs.

   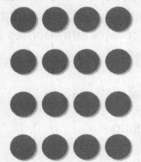

   How many of the songs are pop songs?

   Ⓐ 16
   Ⓑ 12
   Ⓒ 8
   Ⓓ 4

3. Mr. Walton ordered 12 pizzas for the art class celebration. One-fourth of the pizzas had only mushrooms.

   How many of the pizzas had only mushrooms?

   Ⓐ 3   Ⓒ 8
   Ⓑ 4   Ⓓ 9

4. Trisha's mom baked 16 muffins. Two-eighths of the muffins have cranberries.

   How many of the muffins have cranberries?

   Ⓐ 12   Ⓒ 4
   Ⓑ 8   Ⓓ 2

5. Caleb took 24 photos at the zoo. Three-eighths of his photos are of giraffes. Explain how to use a model to find how many photos Caleb took of giraffes.

   _____

   _____

   _____

   _____

Number and Operations–Fractions

1. Gwen uses $\frac{2}{3}$ cup of sugar for one batch of cookies. She used a model to find how much sugar to use in 2 batches of cookies.

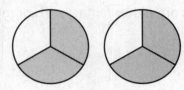

   How much sugar does Gwen need for 2 batches of cookies?

   (A) $1\frac{1}{3}$ cups

   (B) $1\frac{2}{3}$ cups

   (C) $2\frac{1}{3}$ cups

   (D) $2\frac{2}{3}$ cups

2. Brandon used $\frac{3}{4}$ of an 8-ounce package of blueberries to make muffins. How many ounces of blueberries did he use for the muffins? You may use a model to help you solve the problem.

   (A) 2 ounces

   (B) 4 ounces

   (C) 6 ounces

   (D) $7\frac{1}{4}$ ounces

3. Yoshi wants $\frac{3}{5}$ of his garden to have red flowers. His garden has an area of 3 square yards. He used a model to find the area of his garden that will have red flowers.

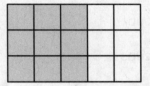

   What area of Yoshi's garden will have red flowers?

   (A) $1\frac{1}{5}$ square yards

   (B) $1\frac{4}{5}$ square yards

   (C) $2\frac{1}{5}$ square yards

   (D) $3\frac{3}{5}$ square yards

4. Kenya needs $\frac{1}{4}$ yard of material to make a placemat. How much material does she need for 6 placemats? You may use a model to help you solve the problem.

   (A) $1\frac{1}{4}$ yards

   (B) $1\frac{1}{2}$ yards

   (C) $1\frac{3}{4}$ yards

   (D) $6\frac{1}{4}$ yards

5. Mike has a 5-pound bag of apples. He will use $\frac{3}{4}$ of the bag to make pies. Explain how to use a model to find how many pounds of apples Mike will use for the pies.

_____

_____

_____

_____

Number and Operations–Fractions

1. Julia has a recipe for salad dressing that calls for $\frac{1}{4}$ cup of sugar. Julia is making 5 batches of the salad dressing. How much sugar will she use?

   (A) $\frac{4}{5}$ cup

   (B) $1\frac{1}{5}$ cups

   (C) $1\frac{1}{4}$ cups

   (D) $5\frac{1}{4}$ cups

2. Taniqua took a test that had 20 questions. She got $\frac{4}{5}$ of the questions correct. How many questions did Taniqua get correct?

   (A) 25

   (B) 16

   (C) 15

   (D) 12

3. In a class book order, $\frac{2}{3}$ of the books are fantasy and $\frac{1}{4}$ of the books are biography. If the order contains 60 books, how many books are either fantasy or biography?

   (A) 15

   (B) 30

   (C) 40

   (D) 55

4. Laurie runs around a track that is $\frac{1}{4}$ mile long. If she does 10 laps around the track, how far does she run?

   (A) $\frac{2}{5}$ mile

   (B) $2\frac{1}{4}$ miles

   (C) $2\frac{1}{2}$ miles

   (D) $10\frac{1}{4}$ miles

5. Mrs. Jackson asked Lance to explain to the class how to find the answer for $9 \times \frac{3}{4}$. How should Lance explain the steps to take to find the answer.

   _____

   _____

   _____

   _____

   _____

   _____

   _____

Number and Operations–Fractions

1. Julia has a recipe for salad dressing that calls for $\frac{3}{4}$ cup of vegetable oil. How much vegetable oil should she use to make $\frac{1}{2}$ of the recipe for salad dressing?

   Ⓐ $1\frac{1}{4}$ cups

   Ⓑ $\frac{2}{3}$ cup

   Ⓒ $\frac{1}{2}$ cup

   Ⓓ $\frac{3}{8}$ cup

3. Of the flowers on Jill's front lawn, $\frac{2}{5}$ are tulips. Of the tulips, $\frac{5}{8}$ are yellow. What fraction of the flowers on Jill's front lawn are yellow tulips?

   Ⓐ $\frac{7}{13}$

   Ⓑ $\frac{1}{2}$

   Ⓒ $\frac{1}{4}$

   Ⓓ $\frac{1}{8}$

2. A scientist had $\frac{3}{4}$ liter of solution. He used $\frac{1}{6}$ of the solution for an experiment. How much solution did the scientist use for the experiment?

   Ⓐ $\frac{1}{8}$ liter

   Ⓑ $\frac{3}{8}$ liter

   Ⓒ $\frac{1}{2}$ liter

   Ⓓ $\frac{7}{12}$ liter

4. Otis bought a total of $\frac{7}{10}$ pound of grapes and cherries. The weight of the grapes is $\frac{2}{3}$ of the total weight. What is the weight of the grapes?

   Ⓐ $\frac{3}{10}$ pound

   Ⓑ $\frac{7}{15}$ pound

   Ⓒ $\frac{9}{13}$ pound

   Ⓓ $\frac{20}{21}$ pound

5. Marni and Leigh shared a pizza. Marni ate $\frac{4}{5}$ of $\frac{5}{12}$ of the pizza. Leigh ate $\frac{1}{2}$ of $\frac{2}{3}$ of the pizza. They both said that they ate the same amount of pizza. Do you agree? Support your answer.

   _____

   _____

   _____

   _____

   _____

   _____

Number and Operations–Fractions

1. Marta breaded $\frac{1}{2}$ of the fish she cooked for dinner. She ate $\frac{1}{3}$ of the breaded fish. She used a model to find how much of the fish she had eaten.

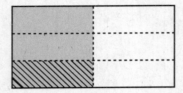

How much of the fish did Marta eat?

Ⓐ $\frac{1}{6}$

Ⓑ $\frac{1}{5}$

Ⓒ $\frac{2}{5}$

Ⓓ $\frac{2}{3}$

2. Lawrence bought $\frac{2}{3}$ pound of roast beef. He used $\frac{3}{4}$ of it to make a sandwich. How much roast beef did Lawrence use for his sandwich? You may use a model to help you solve the problem.

Ⓐ $\frac{5}{12}$ pound

Ⓑ $\frac{1}{2}$ pound

Ⓒ $\frac{5}{7}$ pound

Ⓓ $\frac{6}{7}$ pound

3. Alexa planted tulips in $\frac{2}{5}$ of her garden. Of the tulips, $\frac{2}{3}$ are yellow tulips. She used a model to find what part of her garden has yellow tulips.

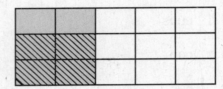

What part of Alexa's garden has yellow tulips?

Ⓐ $\frac{2}{15}$ Ⓒ $\frac{1}{3}$

Ⓑ $\frac{4}{15}$ Ⓓ $\frac{1}{2}$

4. A scientist has a bottle that is $\frac{5}{8}$ full of solution. He uses $\frac{2}{5}$ of the solution in the bottle for an experiment. How much of a full bottle of solution does he use? You may use a model to help you solve the problem.

Ⓐ $\frac{7}{13}$

Ⓑ $\frac{1}{2}$

Ⓒ $\frac{1}{4}$

Ⓓ $\frac{1}{40}$

5. Krista walks $\frac{3}{4}$ mile to school every day. So far today she has walked $\frac{1}{2}$ the distance to school. Explain how to use a model to find how far Krista has walked so far today.

_____

_____

_____

Number and Operations–Fractions

1. Ana has a poster that is $1\frac{2}{3}$ feet high and $2\frac{1}{4}$ feet wide. She used an area model to find the area of the poster.

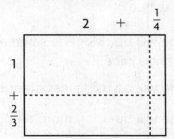

   What is the area of Ana's poster?

   Ⓐ $3\frac{1}{2}$ square feet

   Ⓑ $3\frac{3}{4}$ square feet

   Ⓒ $3\frac{11}{12}$ square feet

   Ⓓ $4\frac{1}{2}$ square feet

2. The top of Colin's desk is $2\frac{2}{3}$ feet long and $2\frac{1}{4}$ feet wide. What is the area of the top of Colin's desk? You may use an area model to help you.

   Ⓐ $4\frac{1}{6}$ square feet

   Ⓑ $4\frac{11}{12}$ square feet

   Ⓒ $5\frac{11}{12}$ square feet

   Ⓓ 6 square feet

3. Eloise is painting a mural that is $1\frac{3}{4}$ yards long and $1\frac{1}{4}$ yards high. She uses a grid to find the area of the mural.

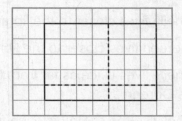

   What is the area of the mural?

   Ⓐ $2\frac{3}{16}$ square yards

   Ⓑ 6 square yards

   Ⓒ $8\frac{3}{4}$ square yards

   Ⓓ 35 square yards

4. A ping pong table is $2\frac{3}{4}$ meters long and $1\frac{1}{2}$ meters wide. What is the area of the ping pong table? You may use an area model to help you.

   Ⓐ $4\frac{1}{8}$ square meters

   Ⓑ $4\frac{1}{4}$ square meters

   Ⓒ $4\frac{3}{8}$ square meters

   Ⓓ $4\frac{1}{2}$ square meters

5. Devon is shopping for a rug for her living room. The rug she likes is $2\frac{1}{2}$ yards long and $1\frac{1}{2}$ yards wide. Explain how Devon can use a grid to find the area of the rug.

   _____

   _____

   _____

1. Doreen lives $\frac{3}{4}$ mile from the library. If Sheila lives $\frac{1}{2}$ as far away as Doreen, which statement below is true?

   (A) Sheila lives closer to the library.

   (B) Doreen lives closer to the library.

   (C) Sheila lives twice as far from the library as Doreen.

   (D) They live the same distance from the library.

2. Mrs. Stephens wrote 4 statements on the board and asked the class which one was true. Which statement below is true?

   (A) $\frac{5}{6} \times \frac{5}{6}$ is equal to $\frac{5}{6}$.

   (B) $\frac{2}{3} \times \frac{1}{3}$ is less than $\frac{2}{3}$.

   (C) $\frac{7}{8} \times 8$ is less than $\frac{7}{8}$.

   (D) $\frac{3}{5} \times 5$ is greater than 5.

3. Nadia needs $\frac{3}{4}$ cup of orange juice for a punch recipe. She will double the recipe to make punch for a party. Which statement below is true?

   (A) She will be using the same amount of orange juice.

   (B) She will be using less orange juice.

   (C) She will be using more orange juice.

   (D) She will be using $\frac{3}{4}$ as much orange juice.

4. It took Mary Lou $\frac{5}{6}$ hour to write a report for her English class. It took Heather $\frac{9}{10}$ as much time to write her report as it took Mary Lou. Which statement below is true?

   (A) It took them both the same amount of time.

   (B) Mary Lou spent less time writing her book report than Heather.

   (C) Mary Lou spent more time writing her book report than Heather.

   (D) It took Heather twice as long to write her book report than it took Mary Lou to write her book report.

5. Dwayne will multiply a recipe for brownies by 4. If the recipe calls for $\frac{1}{3}$ cup of oil, will he need more than or less than $\frac{1}{3}$ cup of oil to make all the brownies? Explain your answer.

_____
_____
_____

Number and Operations–Fractions

1. Stuart rode his bicycle $6\frac{3}{5}$ miles last week. This week he rode $1\frac{1}{3}$ times as far as he rode last week. Which statement below is true?

   Ⓐ He rode the same number of miles both weeks.

   Ⓑ He rode fewer miles this week.

   Ⓒ He rode more miles this week.

   Ⓓ He rode twice as many miles this week.

2. Mrs. Thompson is buying $1\frac{3}{4}$ pounds of turkey and $\frac{3}{4}$ as much cheese as turkey at a deli. Which statement below is true?

   Ⓐ She is buying the same amount of turkey and cheese.

   Ⓑ She is buying less turkey than cheese.

   Ⓒ She is buying twice as much turkey as cheese.

   Ⓓ She is buying more turkey than cheese.

3. Miss Parks wrote 4 statements on the board and asked the class which one was true. Which statement below is true?

   Ⓐ $3\frac{2}{3} \times \frac{4}{5}$ is greater than $3\frac{2}{3}$.

   Ⓑ $1\frac{7}{8} \times 2\frac{1}{3}$ is greater than $2\frac{1}{3}$.

   Ⓒ $2\frac{5}{6} \times \frac{8}{8}$ is less than $2\frac{5}{6}$.

   Ⓓ $2\frac{3}{8} \times 4$ is less than 4.

4. Diana worked on her science project for $5\frac{1}{3}$ hours. Gabe worked on his science project $1\frac{1}{4}$ times as long as Diana. Which statement below is true?

   Ⓐ Gabe spent more time on his science project than Diana did on hers.

   Ⓑ Diana worked on her science project longer than Gabe worked on his.

   Ⓒ Gabe worked on his science project twice as long as Diana worked on hers.

   Ⓓ They both worked on their science projects the same amount of time.

5. Kyleigh has a recipe for punch that calls for $2\frac{1}{4}$ cups of sherbet. If she uses $1\frac{2}{3}$ of that amount, will she be using *more than*, *less than*, or the *same* amount of sherbet? Support your answer.

   _____

   _____

   _____

   _____

Number and Operations–Fractions

1. Louis wants to carpet the rectangular floor of his basement. The basement has an area of 864 square feet. The width of the basement is $\frac{2}{3}$ its length. What is the length of Louis's basement?

   Ⓐ 24 feet

   Ⓑ 36 feet

   Ⓒ 48 feet

   Ⓓ 576 feet

2. Sally painted a picture that has an area of 480 square inches. The length of the painting is $1\frac{1}{5}$ as long as it is wide. Which of the following could be the dimensions of Sally's painting?

   Ⓐ 20 inches by 24 inches

   Ⓑ 12 inches by 40 inches

   Ⓒ 16 inches by 30 inches

   Ⓓ 15 inches by 32 inches

3. A rectangular park has an area of 6 square miles. The width of the property is $\frac{3}{8}$ the length of the property. What is the width of the property?

   Ⓐ $1\frac{1}{2}$ miles

   Ⓑ $2\frac{1}{4}$ miles

   Ⓒ 3 miles

   Ⓓ 4 miles

4. A pool at a park takes up an area of 540 square yards. The length is $1\frac{2}{3}$ times as long as the width. Which of the following could be the dimensions of the pool?

   Ⓐ 21 yards by 35 yards

   Ⓑ 20 yards by 27 yards

   Ⓒ 15 yards by 36 yards

   Ⓓ 18 yards by 30 yards

5. Brianna has a rug that has an area of 24 square feet. The width of the rug is $\frac{2}{3}$ the length of the rug. Explain how you can find the length and the width of the rug.

_____

_____

_____

_____

_____

_____

_____

Number and Operations–Fractions

1. Jared made $12\frac{3}{4}$ cups of snack mix for a party. His guests ate $\frac{2}{3}$ of the mix. How much snack mix did his guests eat?

   (A) $4\frac{5}{12}$ cups

   (A) $4\frac{1}{2}$ cups

   (C) $8\frac{1}{2}$ cups

   (D) $12\frac{5}{7}$ cups

2. Kayla walks $3\frac{7}{10}$ miles for exercise each day. What is the total number of miles she walks in 31 days?

   (A) $117\frac{4}{10}$ miles

   (B) $114\frac{7}{10}$ miles

   (C) $34\frac{7}{10}$ miles

   (D) $6\frac{4}{5}$ miles

3. Carlos has $7\frac{1}{2}$ acres of farmland. He uses $\frac{1}{3}$ of the acres to graze animals and $\frac{1}{5}$ of the acres to grow vegetables. How many acres does Carlos use for grazing animals or for growing vegetables?

   (A) $1\frac{1}{2}$ acres   (C) 4 acres

   (B) $2\frac{1}{2}$ acres   (D) $6\frac{29}{30}$ acres

4. The table shows how many hours some students worked on their math project.

   Math Project

Name	Hours Worked
Carl	$5\frac{1}{4}$
Sonia	$6\frac{1}{2}$
Tony	$5\frac{2}{3}$

   April worked $1\frac{1}{2}$ times as long on her math project as Carl. For how many hours did April work on her math project?

   (A) $5\frac{3}{8}$ hours   (C) $7\frac{1}{4}$ hours

   (B) $6\frac{1}{3}$ hours   (D) $7\frac{7}{8}$ hours

5. Jessica rides the bus $8\frac{4}{5}$ miles each day. Explain how to use the Distributive Property to find the total number of miles Jessica rides in 20 days.

   _____

   _____

   _____

   _____

   _____

1. Olivia needs to find the number of $\frac{1}{3}$-cup servings in 2 cups of rice. She used the number line below to find $2 \div \frac{1}{3}$.

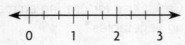

How many $\frac{1}{3}$-cup servings of rice are in 2 cups of rice?

(A) 2

(B) 3

(C) 5

(D) 6

2. Kwami bought 8 yards of lanyard. He cut the lanyard into $\frac{1}{2}$-yard pieces. How many pieces of lanyard did Kwami make?

(A) 2

(B) 8

(C) 16

(D) 64

3. Chris divided $\frac{1}{2}$ pound of nails into 6 small bags with the same amount in each bag. He used fraction strips to find the weight of each bag.

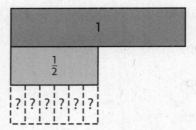

How much does each small bag weigh?

(A) $\frac{1}{2}$ pound

(B) $\frac{1}{3}$ pound

(C) $\frac{1}{6}$ pound

(D) $\frac{1}{12}$ pound

4. Josie filled a watering can with $\frac{1}{3}$ quart of water. She poured the same amount of water from the can onto each of 3 plants. How much water did Josie pour onto each plant?

(A) $\frac{1}{9}$ quart

(B) $2\frac{2}{3}$ quarts

(C) 3 quarts

(D) 9 quarts

5. Four athletes shared $\frac{1}{2}$ gallon of sports drink equally. Explain how to use fraction strips to find how much sports drink each athlete got.

_____

_____

_____

_____

Number and Operations–Fractions

1. Ben is making a recipe that calls for 5 cups of flour. He only has a $\frac{1}{2}$-cup measuring cup. How many times will Ben need to fill the $\frac{1}{2}$-cup measuring cup to get 5 cups of flour?

   (A) $\frac{2}{5}$

   (B) $2\frac{1}{2}$

   (C) 7

   (D) 10

2. Lily made 3 pounds of coleslaw for a picnic. Each serving of coleslaw is $\frac{1}{8}$ pound. How many $\frac{1}{8}$-pound servings of coleslaw are there?

   (A) $2\frac{2}{3}$

   (B) 12

   (C) 24

   (D) 32

3. Kyle shares 3 bananas with some friends. If each person gets $\frac{1}{2}$ of a banana, how many people can share Kyle's bananas?

   (A) 9

   (B) 6

   (C) $1\frac{1}{2}$

   (D) $\frac{1}{6}$

4. A 6-mile walking trail has a distance marker every $\frac{1}{3}$ mile, beginning at $\frac{1}{3}$ mile. How many distance markers are along the trail?

   (A) 2

   (B) 6

   (C) 9

   (D) 18

5. Aya made 2 pans of brownies to give to some families in her neighborhood. Each family will get $\frac{1}{4}$ of a pan. How many families will share Aya's brownies? Explain how to use a diagram to find your answer.

   _____

   _____

   _____

   _____

   _____

Number and Operations–Fractions

1. Samara solved $\frac{1}{5} \div 10$ by using a related multiplication sentence. Which multiplication sentence could she have used?

   (A) $5 \times 10 = 50$

   (B) $\frac{1}{5} \times 10 = 2$

   (C) $5 \times \frac{1}{10} = \frac{5}{10}$

   (D) $\frac{1}{5} \times \frac{1}{10} = \frac{1}{50}$

2. Jawan solved $8 \div \frac{1}{3}$ by using a related multiplication sentence. Which multiplication sentence could he have used?

   (A) $8 \times \frac{1}{3} = \frac{8}{3}$

   (B) $\frac{1}{8} \times \frac{1}{3} = \frac{1}{24}$

   (C) $8 \times 3 = 24$

   (D) $\frac{1}{8} \times 3 = \frac{3}{8}$

3. Annette has $\frac{1}{4}$ pound of cheese that she is going to cut into 3 chunks of the same size. What fraction of a pound of cheese will each chunk be?

   (A) $\frac{1}{12}$ pound

   (B) $\frac{1}{8}$ pound

   (C) $\frac{1}{2}$ pound

   (D) $\frac{3}{4}$ pound

4. Eli made 2 peanut butter and jelly sandwiches and cut each one into fourths. How many $\frac{1}{4}$-sandwich pieces did Eli have?

   (A) $\frac{1}{8}$

   (B) $2\frac{1}{4}$

   (C) 4

   (D) 8

5. Miss Becker asked her class to write a division expression using a whole number and a unit fraction that will have a quotient greater than its dividend. Cassie wrote $\frac{1}{2} \div 6$. Explain why Cassie is incorrect. Then give a correct expression.

_____

_____

_____

_____

Number and Operations–Fractions

1. Tina has $\frac{1}{2}$ quart of iced tea. She pours the same amount into each of 3 glasses. Which equation represents the fraction of a quart of iced tea, n, that is in each glass?

   (A) $\frac{1}{2} \div \frac{1}{3} = n$

   (B) $\frac{1}{2} \div 3 = n$

   (C) $3 \div \frac{1}{2} = n$

   (D) $3 \div 2 = n$

2. Lucy bought 9 yards of ribbon on a spool. She cut the ribbon into $\frac{1}{2}$-yard pieces. Which equation represents the number of pieces of ribbon, n, Lucy has now?

   (A) $9 \div \frac{1}{2} = n$

   (B) $\frac{1}{2} \div 9 = n$

   (C) $2 \div 9 = n$

   (D) $9 \div 2 = n$

3. Which situation can be represented by $6 \div \frac{1}{3}$?

   (A) Rita has a piece of ribbon that is $\frac{1}{3}$ foot long. She cuts it into 6 pieces, each having the same length. How many feet long is each piece of ribbon?

   (B) Rita has 6 pieces of ribbon. Each piece is $\frac{1}{3}$ foot long. How many feet of ribbon does Rita have in all?

   (C) Rita has a piece of ribbon that is 6 feet long. She cuts it into pieces that are $\frac{1}{3}$ foot long. How many pieces of ribbon does Rita have?

   (D) Rita has a piece of ribbon that is 6 feet long. She cuts it into 3 pieces. How many feet long is each piece of ribbon?

4. Mrs. Green wrote the following equation on the board. $2 \div \frac{1}{3} = n$. Scott wrote this situation to represent the equation: Lisa and Frank shared $\frac{1}{3}$ pound of cherries equally. What fractional part of a pound did each one get?

   Does Scott's situation represent the equation? Support you answer.

   _____

   _____

   _____

   _____

   _____

   _____

Number and Operations–Fractions

1. The first stop on a bus route is 4 miles from school. How many yards are in 4 miles?

   Ⓐ   48 yards

   Ⓑ   144 yards

   Ⓒ   7,040 yards

   Ⓓ   21,120 yards

2. Anoki bought 36 yards of fabric to make costumes for the school play. What is that length in inches?

   Ⓐ   3 inches

   Ⓑ   12 inches

   Ⓒ   108 inches

   Ⓓ   1,296 inches

3. Sarah is 53 inches tall. Sarah's brother Luke is 4 inches taller than she is. What is Luke's height in feet and inches?

   Ⓐ   4 feet 7 inches

   Ⓑ   4 feet 9 inches

   Ⓒ   5 feet 7 inches

   Ⓓ   5 feet 8 inches

4. The distance between a football field and a parking lot is 135 feet. What is that length in yards?

   Ⓐ   36 yards

   Ⓑ   45 yards

   Ⓒ   405 yards

   Ⓓ   1,620 yards

5. The distance between second and third bases on a regulation baseball field is 90 feet. Scott says he needs to multiply to find the number of yards between second and third bases. Do you agree? Support your answer.

   _____

   _____

   _____

   _____

   _____

   _____

Measurement and Data

1. Brian filled 72 glasses with apple juice for a school party. If each glass holds 1 cup of juice, how many quarts of apple juice did Brian use?

   Ⓐ   9 quarts
   Ⓑ   18 quarts
   Ⓒ   36 quarts
   Ⓓ 288 quarts

2. Mrs. Davis has 64 bottles of water. If each bottle holds 1 pint of water, how many gallons of water does Mrs. Davis have?

   Ⓐ   4 gallons
   Ⓑ   6 gallons
   Ⓒ   8 gallons
   Ⓓ 32 gallons

3. Isabel bought 3 bottles of liquid soap. Each bottle has 1 quart of soap in it. How many fluid ounces of liquid soap are in the 3 bottles that Isabel bought?

   Ⓐ 16 fluid ounces
   Ⓑ 32 fluid ounces
   Ⓒ 72 fluid ounces
   Ⓓ 96 fluid ounces

4. Mark filled 48 glasses with orange juice for a camp breakfast. If each glass holds 1 cup of juice, how many quarts of orange juice did Mark use?

   Ⓐ   6 quarts
   Ⓑ 12 quarts
   Ⓒ 24 quarts
   Ⓓ 192 quarts

5. Beth filled 32 jars with paint. Each jar holds 1 pint of paint. Beth found that she needed 4 gallons of paint to fill the jars by converting more than once. Describe how Beth converted from pints to gallons.

   _____

   _____

   _____

   _____

   _____

Measurement and Data

1. Students picked 576 ounces of apples to make apple cider. How many pounds of apples did they pick?

   (A) 16 pounds

   (B) 36 pounds

   (C) 48 pounds

   (D) 9,216 pounds

2. Keiko bought 3 pounds of fruit salad. How many ounces of fruit salad did Keiko buy?

   (A) 16 ounces

   (B) 32 ounces

   (C) 36 ounces

   (D) 48 ounces

3. A female elephant can weigh up to 8,000 pounds. What is this weight in tons?

   (A) 2 tons

   (B) 3 tons

   (C) 4 tons

   (D) 8 tons

4. A truck loaded with concrete weighs about 30 tons. What is this weight in pounds?

   (A) 30,000 pounds

   (B) 60,000 pounds

   (C) 300,000 pounds

   (D) 600,000 pounds

5. Seth bought 3 pounds of grapes. Maritza bought 50 ounces of grapes. Whose grapes weighed more? Explain how you know.

_____

_____

_____

_____

_____

_____

1. At the bulk food store, Stacey bought 7 pounds of nuts. She used 8 ounces of nuts in a recipe and then made small bags to use for snacks. If each small bag contained 4 ounces of nuts, how many small bags of nuts did Stacey make?

   (A) 15
   (B) 19
   (C) 26
   (D) 29

2. Keisha is walking around a track that is 400 yards long. She has walked around the track 5 times so far. How many more yards does she need to walk around the track to do 2 miles?

   (A) 1,520 yards
   (B) 3,120 yards
   (C) 3,280 yards
   (D) 8,560 yards

3. Devon uses 64 inches of ribbon to make 1 bow. How many yards of ribbon does Devon need to make 9 bows?

   (A) 8 yards
   (B) 16 yards
   (C) 24 yards
   (D) 48 yards

4. Brandon bought a 5-gallon container of paint to paint his house. After he finished painting, he had 2 quarts of paint left over. How many quarts of paint did Brandon use?

   (A) 3 quarts
   (B) 8 quarts
   (C) 18 quarts
   (D) 23 quarts

5. Vincent needs 30 inches of wood to make a shelf. Vincent says he needs 15 feet of wood to make 6 shelves. Do you agree? Support your answer.

   _____

   _____

   _____

   _____

   _____

Measurement and Data

1. Ed bought 3 liters of water, 2,750 milliliters of sports drink, and 2.25 liters of juice. Which statement is true?

   (A) Ed bought 50 milliliters more sports drink than juice.

   (B) Ed bought 1.25 liters more water than juice.

   (C) Ed bought 75 milliliters more water than juice.

   (D) Ed bought 250 milliliters more water than sports drink.

2. Roland's dog has a mass of 2,500 dekagrams. What is the dog's mass in kilograms?

   (A)　　0.25 kilogram

   (B)　　2.5 kilograms

   (C)　　25 kilograms

   (D) 250 kilograms

3. Sofia bought 3.25 meters of fabric to make a costume. How many centimeters of fabric did she buy?

   (A)　　0.325 centimeter

   (B)　　3.25 centimeters

   (C)　　32.5 centimeters

   (D) 325 centimeters

4. Lorena's backpack has a mass of 10,000 grams. What is the mass of Lorena's backpack in kilograms?

   (A)　　1 kilogram

   (B)　　10 kilograms

   (C)　　100 kilograms

   (D) 1,000 kilograms

5. Richard can walk at a rate of 5 kilometers in an hour. Explain how to find how many meters Richard can walk in an hour. Then find how many meters he walks in an hour.

   _____

   _____

   _____

   _____

Measurement and Data

1. When it is full, a fish tank holds 15 gallons of water. Jordan is using a 1-pint container to fill the fish tank. How many times will he need to fill the 1-pint container to fill the fish tank?

   Ⓐ 30
   Ⓑ 60
   Ⓒ 90
   Ⓓ 120

2. An art teacher has a roll of art paper 5 meters long. She needs to cut it into 1-decimeter long pieces for a collage project. How many 1-decimeter pieces can she cut from the roll of art paper?

   Ⓐ 5
   Ⓑ 50
   Ⓒ 500
   Ⓓ 5,000

3. Mickey needs to cut pieces of ribbon that are each 1 meter long to tie onto balloons. If he has 8 pieces of ribbon that are each 1 dekameter long, how many 1-meter pieces of ribbon can he cut?

   Ⓐ 80
   Ⓑ 800
   Ⓒ 8,000
   Ⓓ 80,000

4. The largest known carnivorous dinosaur, Spinosaurus, weighed about 18,000 pounds. How many tons did the Spinosaurus dinosaur weigh?

   Ⓐ 9 tons
   Ⓑ 18 tons
   Ⓒ 36 tons
   Ⓓ 90 tons

5. A Komodo dragon lizard can grow up to about 30 decimeters in length. Toni says that this is 300 centimeters. Do you agree? Explain how you can use a table to support your answer.

   _____
   _____
   _____
   _____
   _____
   _____
   _____

1. The high school football game started at 7:15 P.M. and ended at 10:44 P.M. How long did the game last?

   (A) 2 hours 9 minutes

   (B) 2 hours 29 minutes

   (C) 3 hours 9 minutes

   (D) 3 hours 29 minutes

2. Betsy spent 26 days traveling in Europe. How many weeks and days did Betsy travel in Europe?

   (A) 2 weeks 6 days

   (B) 3 weeks 5 days

   (C) 4 weeks 2 days

   (D) 5 weeks 1 day

3. Students arrived at the science museum at 1:15 P.M. They stayed at the museum for 2 hours 51 minutes. What time did the students leave the museum?

   (A) 3:06 P.M.

   (B) 4:00 P.M.

   (C) 4:06 P.M.

   (D) 4:44 P.M.

4. It takes Kate 10 minutes to walk to the bus stop. How many seconds does it take her to walk to the bus stop?

   (A) 6,000 seconds

   (B) 600 seconds

   (C) 60 seconds

   (D) 6 seconds

5. The Diaz family arrived for breakfast at a diner at 8:45 A.M. They stayed at the diner for 1 hour 23 minutes. What time did the family leave the diner? Explain how you found your answer.

   _____

   _____

   _____

   _____

Measurement and Data

Use the line plot for 1–2.

Maya measured the heights of the seedlings she was growing. She made a line plot to record the data.

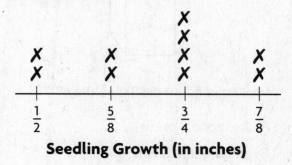

Seedling Growth (in inches)

1. What was the total growth, in inches, of Maya's seedlings?

   (A) 3 inches   (C) 7 inches

   (B) $3\frac{1}{2}$ inches   (D) 10 inches

2. What was the average height, in inches, of the seedlings she measured?

   (A) $\frac{11}{16}$ inch   (C) $\frac{3}{4}$ inch

   (B) $\frac{7}{10}$ inch   (D) $\frac{7}{8}$ inch

Use the line plot for 3–4.

A builder is buying property where she can build new houses. The line plot shows the sizes of the lots for each house.

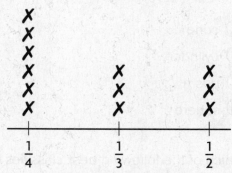

House Lots (in acres)

3. How many acres does the builder buy?

   (A) 3 acres   (C) 6 acres

   (B) 4 acres   (D) 12 acres

4. What is the average size of the lots?

   (A) $\frac{1}{12}$ acre   (C) $\frac{1}{4}$ acre

   (B) $\frac{1}{6}$ acre   (D) $\frac{1}{3}$ acre

---

5. Shia measured the thickness of the buttons in her collection. She graphed the results in a line plot.

   What steps could Shia use to find the average thickness of her buttons?

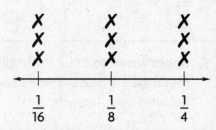

Button Thicknesses (in inches)

_____

_____

1. Koji is building a tower out of paper. He starts by making 2 congruent circular bases. He then makes 1 curved surface for the body of the tower. What three-dimensional figure does Koji build?

   (A) cone

   (B) cylinder

   (C) prism

   (D) sphere

2. Which of the following **best** classifies this solid figure?

   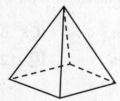

   (A) triangular pyramid

   (B) triangular prism

   (C) square pyramid

   (D) square prism

3. Tanya drew this solid figure on her notebook.

   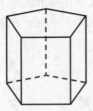

   What solid figure did Tanya draw?

   (A) hexagonal prism

   (B) pentagonal prism

   (C) hexagonal pyramid

   (D) pentagonal pyramid

4. Min Soo is making solid figures in the shape of party hats. He starts by making 1 circular base. He then makes 1 curved surface for the figure. What three-dimensional figure does Min Soo make?

   (A) prism

   (B) sphere

   (C) cylinder

   (D) cone

5. Randi wants to draw three-dimensional figures whose lateral faces are all rectangles. She says she can draw prisms **and** pyramids. Do you agree? Support your answer.

   _____

   _____

   _____

   _____

Measurement and Data

1. Chase built a solid figure with unit cubes. How many unit cubes did he use for his figure?

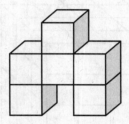

Ⓐ 5
Ⓑ 6
Ⓒ 7
Ⓓ 8

2. Diana used more than one unit cube to build a figure. When she traced around the figure, she drew a square. What is the **least** number of unit cubes she could have used?

Ⓐ 1
Ⓑ 2
Ⓒ 4
Ⓓ 9

3. Ella placed some unit cubes on her desk as shown below. How many unit cubes did Ella use?

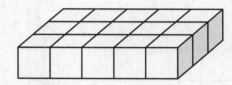

Ⓐ 5
Ⓑ 10
Ⓒ 15
Ⓓ 20

4. Henry stacked these unit cubes. How many unit cubes did Henry stack?

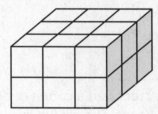

Ⓐ 6
Ⓑ 9
Ⓒ 12
Ⓓ 18

5. Kamal has 24 unit cubes. He says he can build 8 different rectangular prisms with the cubes. Do you agree? Support your answer.

_____

_____

1. Cole stacked 1-foot cube-shaped boxes in a storage bin as shown. What is the volume of the space he filled?

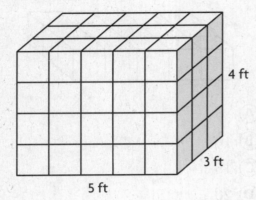

4 ft

3 ft

5 ft

Each cube = 1 cu ft

Ⓐ 20 cu in.

Ⓑ 20 cu ft

Ⓒ 60 cu in.

Ⓓ 60 cu ft

2. A jeweler received a carton of boxes packed with gift boxes. The gift boxes were 2 inches long on each edge. If 12 boxes completely fill the carton, what is the volume of the carton?

Ⓐ 24 cu in.

Ⓑ 48 cu in.

Ⓒ 96 cu in.

Ⓓ 144 cu in.

3. Lindsay filled a box with 1-centimeter cubes. What is the volume of box?

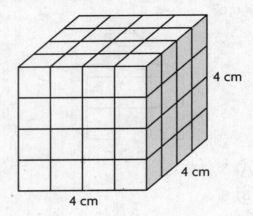

4 cm

4 cm

4 cm

Each cube = 1 cu cm

Ⓐ 16 cu cm   Ⓒ 64 cu cm

Ⓑ 16 cu m   Ⓓ 64 cu m

4. Marina packed 36 1-inch cubes into this box. How many layers of cubes did Marina make?

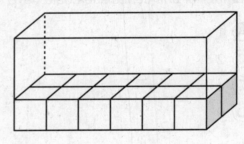

Ⓐ 2   Ⓒ 4

Ⓑ 3   Ⓓ 6

5. Marcy used 1-inch blocks to build a cube whose edges are 3 inches long. Landon used 1-inch blocks to build a cube whose edges are 6 inches long. Landon says his cube has twice the volume of Marcy's cube. Is Landon correct? Support your answer.

_____

_____

_____

1. The volume of a box of coloring pencils is 250 cubic centimeters. Which is the best estimate of the volume of the box that the coloring pencils came packed in?

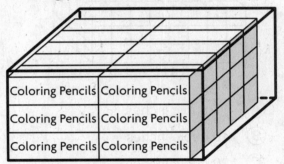

- (A) 750 cu cm
- (C) 7,500 cu cm
- (B) 3,750 cu cm
- (D) 75,000 cu cm

2. Joe packed boxes of staplers into a larger box. If the volume of each stapler box is 400 cubic centimeters, which is the best estimate for the volume of the box that Joe packed with staplers?

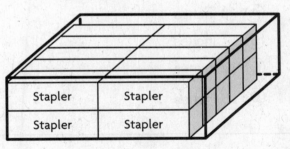

- (A) 800 cu cm
- (C) 4,000 cu cm
- (B) 2,000 cu cm
- (D) 8,000 cu cm

3. The volume of a pencil box is 80 cubic inches. Which is the best estimate of the volume of the box that the pencil boxes came packed in?

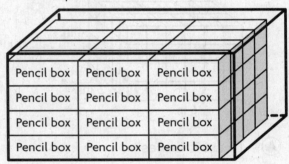

- (A) 9,600 cu in.
- (C) 960 cu in.
- (B) 3,840 cu in.
- (D) 384 cu in.

4. Joe packed tissue boxes into a larger box. If the volume of each tissue box is 90 cubic inches, which is the best estimate for the volume of the box that Joe packed with tissue boxes?

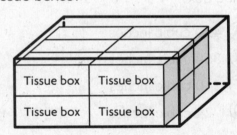

- (A) 360 cu in.
- (C) 720 cu in.
- (B) 540 cu in.
- (D) 1,080 cu in.

5. Janelle is trying to decide which of two shipping boxes has the greater volume. Explain how Janelle can compare the volumes of the shipping box using small boxes.

_____

_____

_____

_____

Measurement and Data

1. Claudine filled a box with smaller boxes shaped like cubes. What is the volume of the box Claudine filled?

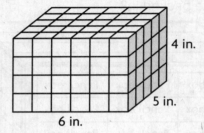

4 in.
5 in.
6 in.

- (A) 15 cubic inches
- (B) 25 cubic inches
- (C) 100 cubic inches
- (D) 120 cubic inches

2. Luke keeps his art supplies in a shoe box that is 12 inches long, 7 inches wide, and 5 inches high. What is the volume of the shoe box?

- (A) 420 cubic inches
- (B) 358 cubic inches
- (C) 240 cubic inches
- (D) 24 cubic inches

3. Barbie stacked small cubes into a box until it was full. What is the volume of the box?

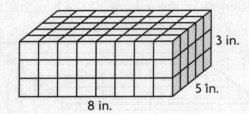

3 in.
5 in.
8 in.

- (A) 18 cubic inches
- (B) 40 cubic inches
- (C) 120 cubic inches
- (D) 158 cubic inches

4. A storage bin in the shape of a rectangular prism has a volume of 5,400 cubic inches. The base area of the storage bin is 450 square inches. What is the height of the storage bin?

- (A) 9 inches
- (B) 11 inches
- (C) 12 inches
- (D) 15 inches

5. Melissa wants to know the volume of a box that is 4 inches long, 2 inches wide, and 5 inches tall. Explain how Melissa can use cubes to find the volume of the box.

_____

_____

_____

_____

_____

Measurement and Data

1. Antonio found an antique chest in his grandfather's attic.

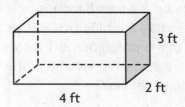

3 ft
2 ft
4 ft

What is the volume of the chest?

(A) 6 cubic feet   (C) 12 cubic feet

(B) 9 cubic feet   (D) 24 cubic feet

2. When Emma went to college, her mother packed up all her old skiing trophies into a box with the dimensions shown.

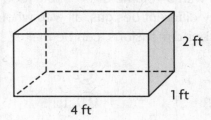

2 ft
1 ft
4 ft

What is the volume of the box?

(A) 7 cubic feet   (C) 9 cubic feet

(B) 8 cubic feet   (D) 10 cubic feet

3. Kristin keeps paper clips in a box that is the shape of a cube. Each edge of the cube is 3 inches. What is the volume of the cube?

(A) 6 cubic inches

(B) 9 cubic inches

(C) 18 cubic inches

(D) 27 cubic inches

4. Will moved a box of old newspapers from the back room of the library.

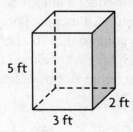

5 ft
2 ft
3 ft

What is the volume of the box?

(A) 10 cubic feet

(B) 15 cubic feet

(C) 30 cubic feet

(D) 40 cubic feet

5. Tom keeps sticky notes in a box that is the shape of a cube. Each edge of the cube is 4 inches. Tom says that the volume of the cube is 16 cubic inches. Is Tom correct? Explain.

_____

_____

_____

_____

1. Ben is filling a box that has the shape of a rectangular prism with 1-inch cubes. A layer of 7 rows with 8 cubes in each row filled the bottom of the box. The volume of the box is 224 cubic inches. How many layers of cubes can Ben fit in the box?

Ⓐ 2   Ⓒ 8

Ⓑ 4   Ⓓ 10

2. Mary bought a puzzle in a box that has a width of 3 inches, a length of 10 inches, and a height of 8 inches. She put it in a box that has a volume of 576 cubic inches so she could mail it with some other things. How many cubic inches of space were left in the box?

Ⓐ 816 cu in.   Ⓒ 336 cu in.

Ⓑ 597 cu in.   Ⓓ 240 cu in.

3. Sylvia can buy a blue box or a green box to store her markers. Both boxes have a base that measures 8 inches by 4 inches. The height of the blue box is 2 inches. The height of the green box is 1 inch. How much greater is the volume of the blue box than the green box?

Ⓐ 96 cu in.   Ⓒ 35 cu in.

Ⓑ 64 cu in.   Ⓓ 32 cu in.

4. Mr. McDonald is designing a cabinet to store sports equipment in the gym. The length and width of one design cannot be the same as the length or width of another design. He wants the cabinet to be 5 feet high with a volume of 60 cubic feet. How many different designs, all with whole number dimensions, can he make?

Ⓐ 2   Ⓒ 6

Ⓑ 3   Ⓓ 12

5. Margie is packing 108 small boxes into a large carton. The small boxes will fill all of the space inside the large carton. Each small box is 3 inches long, 2 inches wide, and 1 inch high. The width of the base and the height of the large carton are the same. The length of the base is less than 36 inches. All of the dimensions are whole numbers. Explain how to find possible dimensions for the large carton.

_____

_____

_____

_____

_____

_____

1. Dmitri built a step out of blocks. What is the volume of the step?

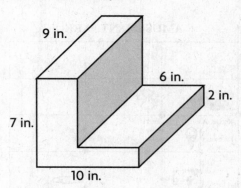

9 in.

6 in.

2 in.

7 in.

10 in.

Ⓐ 360 cu in.　　Ⓒ 540 cu in.

Ⓑ 450 cu in.　　Ⓓ 750 cu in.

2. Latoya built some new steps up to the front of her house. What is the volume of the steps?

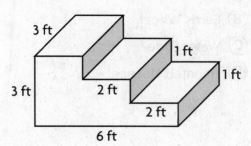

3 ft

1 ft

3 ft　2 ft

1 ft

2 ft

6 ft

Ⓐ 18 cu ft　　Ⓒ 48 cu ft

Ⓑ 36 cu ft　　Ⓓ 54 cu ft

3. Maksim built a scratching toy for his cat. What is the volume of the scratching toy?

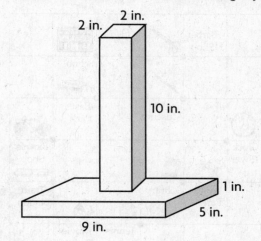

2 in.　2 in.

10 in.

1 in.

9 in.　5 in.

Ⓐ　85 cu in.　　Ⓒ　210 cu in.

Ⓑ 180 cu in.　　Ⓓ 1,800 cu in.

4. Jacinda made some steps for her deck. What is the volume of the steps?

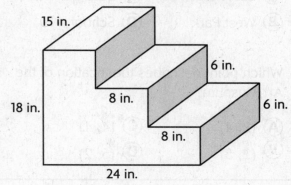

15 in.

6 in.

8 in.

6 in.

18 in.

8 in.

6 in.

24 in.

Ⓐ　　432 cu in.　　Ⓒ 4,320 cu in.

Ⓑ 3,240 cu in.　　Ⓓ 6,480 cu in.

5. Look at the step in problem 1. Explain how to find the volume of the step by subtraction.

_____

_____

_____

Use the coordinate grid for 1–2.

Lindsey made a map of her town.

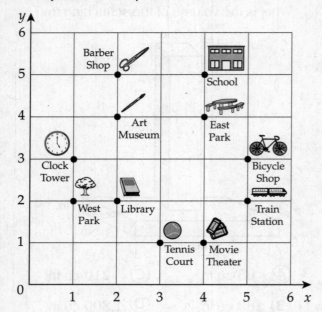

Use the coordinate grid for 3–4.

The map shows the location of the attractions in an amusement park.

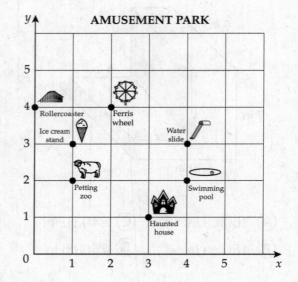

1. Which place in Lindsey's town is located at (4, 5)?

   (A) East Park   (C) Barber Shop

   (B) West Park   (D) School

2. Which point describes the location of the Art Museum?

   (A) (2, 4)   (C) (4, 4)

   (B) (2, 5)   (D) (5, 2)

3. Which attraction is located at (2, 4)?

   (A) Rollercoaster

   (B) Ferris Wheel

   (C) Water Slide

   (D) Haunted Houses

4. In the map of the amusement park above, how far apart are the Petting Zoo and the Swimming Pool? Explain how you found your answer.

   _____

   _____

   _____

   _____

Geometry

Use the graph for 1–3.

Sunil made this graph to show the weight of his new puppy.

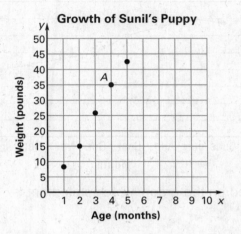

Growth of Sunil's Puppy

1. At what age did the puppy weigh 26 pounds?

   (A) 2 months   (C) 3 months

   (B) 4 months   (D) 5 months

2. What information is represented by the point labeled *A*?

   (A) The puppy weighed 4 pounds at age 35 months.

   (B) The puppy weighed 40 pounds at age 4 months.

   (C) The puppy weighed 35 pounds at age 4 months.

   (D) The puppy weighed 35 pounds at age 5 months.

3. What was the weight of the puppy at age 5 months?

   (A) 40 pounds   (C) 47 pounds

   (B) 43 pounds   (D) 50 pounds

4. Meredith made a table to show how much she read over four days.

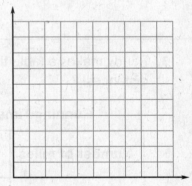

Meredith's Reading Progress				
Day	1	2	3	4
Total Number of Pages	19	42	60	85

Use the table to show the data on a coordinate grid. Give the grid a title and plot a point for each ordered pair in the table. Would the ordered pair (5, 21) make sense on the graph? Explain your answer.

_____

_____

_____

_____

1. Kareem made a table showing how much he earned each month mowing lawns.

Lawn Mowing Earnings

Month	April	May	June	July	August
Amount Earned	$40	$55	$60	$75	$50

What are the most appropriate scale and interval for Kareem to use to make a line graph of the data?

(A) Scale: 0 to 50, Interval: 2

(B) Scale: 0 to 50, Interval: 5

(C) Scale: 0 to 100, Interval: 10

(D) Scale: 0 to 100, Interval: 20

2. A scientist made a line graph that showed how a bear's average heart rate changes over time.

CHANGE IN AVERAGE HEART RATE OF BEARS

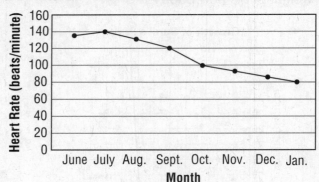

Based on the graph, which statement is true?

(A) A bear's average heart rate rarely changes.

(B) A bear's average heart rate starts to decrease at the end of the summer.

(C) A bear's average heart rate increases over time.

(D) A bear's average heart rate is at its lowest in the summer.

3. Randy makes a table that shows how long it takes her to run different distances.

Running Time and Distance

Number of miles	1	2	3	4
Time (in minutes)	10	20	28	35

Randy uses the data to make a line graph. Describe the line graph.

_____

_____

_____

Geometry

1. Mr. Delgado sees this sign while he is driving.

   Which **best** describes the sign?

   Ⓐ triangle; regular polygon

   Ⓑ triangle; not a regular polygon

   Ⓒ hexagon; regular polygon

   Ⓓ hexagon; not a regular polygon

2. Mr. Diaz is building a fence around his yard. He drew a sketch of the fence line.

   Which **best** describes the fence line?

   Ⓐ pentagon; regular polygon

   Ⓑ pentagon; not a regular polygon

   Ⓒ hexagon; regular polygon

   Ⓓ hexagon; not a regular polygon

3. A stained glass window at the town library is the shape of a regular octagon. Which of the following describes a regular octagon?

   Ⓐ a figure with 6 congruent sides and 6 congruent angles

   Ⓑ a figure with 6 sides that are not congruent

   Ⓒ a figure with 8 sides that are not congruent

   Ⓓ a figure with 8 congruent sides and 8 congruent angles

4. Beth drew four quadrilaterals. Which of the quadrilaterals that she drew is a regular polygon?

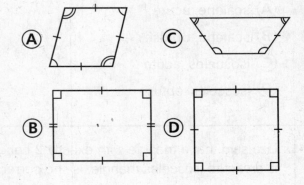

5. Erica drew a rectangle and said that it is a regular polygon because it has four congruent angles. Do you agree? Explain your answer.

   _____

   _____

   _____

   _____

   _____

1. Which kind of triangle has no congruent sides?

   (A) equilateral

   (B) horizontal

   (C) isosceles

   (D) scalene

2. Nathan drew this triangle.

   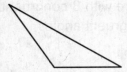

   Which of the following **best** classifies the triangle?

   (A) scalene, acute

   (B) scalene, obtuse

   (C) isosceles, acute

   (D) isosceles, obtuse

3. What is the **least** number of acute angles that a triangle can have?

   (A) 0

   (B) 1

   (C) 2

   (D) 3

4. Amanda drew this triangle.

   Which of the following **best** classifies the triangle?

   (A) equilateral, acute

   (B) isosceles, acute

   (C) scalene, acute

   (D) isosceles, right

5. Liza said that a triangle with exactly 2 congruent sides and a right angle is an acute isosceles triangle. Is she correct? Explain.

   _____

   _____

   _____

1. Keiko drew the shapes of her tables on grid paper. Then she cut them out and used them on a floor plan to help arrange her furniture.

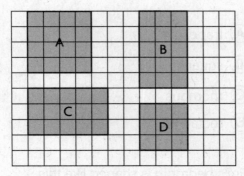

Which two shapes that Keiko drew are congruent?

(A) A and B   (C) B and C

(B) A and C   (D) B and D

2. Ezra drew triangles to make this design.

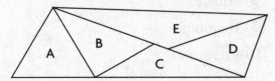

Which of the triangles appear to be congruent?

(A) A and B   (C) C and E

(B) B and D   (D) A and D

3. Fumiko drew the shapes of her neighbors' patios on grid paper.

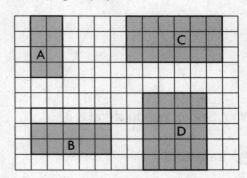

Which two shapes that Fumiko drew are congruent?

(A) A and B   (C) B and C

(B) A and C   (D) B and D

4. Ian drew triangles to make this design.

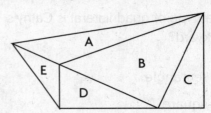

Which of the triangles appear to be congruent?

(A) A and E   (C) B and D

(B) B and C   (D) C and D

5. Juanita has a quadrilateral that she thinks is a rhombus, but she does not have a ruler to measure the sides. How can Juanita determine whether the quadrilateral is a rhombus?

_____

_____

_____

Geometry

1. Jim's vegetable garden looks like this quadrilateral.

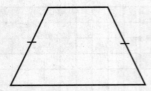

   What type of quadrilateral is it?

   Ⓐ trapezoid
   Ⓑ square
   Ⓒ rhombus
   Ⓓ rectangle

2. Cathy drew a picture of her backyard.

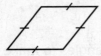

   What type of quadrilateral is Cathy's backyard?

   Ⓐ rectangle
   Ⓑ square
   Ⓒ rhombus
   Ⓓ trapezoid

3. The patio at the front of the school is a quadrilateral with 4 right angles and 4 congruent sides. What type of quadrilateral is it?

   Ⓐ trapezoid
   Ⓑ square
   Ⓒ rhombus
   Ⓓ rectangle

4. Tim's bedroom is shaped like this quadrilateral.

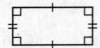

   What type of quadrilateral is it?

   Ⓐ rectangle
   Ⓑ square
   Ⓒ rhombus
   Ⓓ trapezoid

5. Gabrielle drew a quadrilateral with 3 congruent sides. She claims that it must be a rhombus or a square. Is she correct? Explain your answer.

   _____

   _____

   _____

   _____

Geometry

Name _____

Lesson 1
CC.5.OA.1

1. Mr. Perkins used the expression $20 - 10 - 3 \times 2$ to find how much change he should receive. How much change should he receive?

   Ⓐ $2
   Ⓑ $4
   Ⓒ $6
   Ⓓ $14

2. Randy used the expression $2 \times 3 + 3 \times 6 + 1$ to find the number of points the Jaguars scored in all. How many points did the Jaguars score in all?

   Ⓐ 25
   Ⓑ 55
   Ⓒ 73
   Ⓓ 74

3. Amanda used the expression $8 + 25 \times 2 - 45$ to find how many beads she has. How many beads does she have?

   Ⓐ 3
   Ⓑ 13
   Ⓒ 21
   Ⓓ 103

4. Arlene used the expression $3 \times 6 + 2 \times 8 + 1$ to find the number of drinks she bought altogether. How many drinks did she buy altogether?

   Ⓐ 215
   Ⓑ 195
   Ⓒ 36
   Ⓓ 35

5. Brett evaluated the expression $5 + 12 \times 3 + 15 \times 2$ to find the total cost of some CDs. He says the total cost is $81. Explain the error that Brett made and find the correct total cost.

   Possible answer: Brett added first instead of multiplying. The correct order should be $5 + (12 \times 3) + (15 \times 2)$. The correct total cost is $71.

Operations and Algebraic Thinking   1

Name _____

Lesson 2
CC.5.OA.1

1. Meredith and her brother Liam are saving to buy a basketball hoop that costs $75. Meredith earns $15 per week for babysitting and spends $6 of it. Liam earns $10 per week for walking dogs and spends $4 of it. Which expression can be used to find out how many weeks it will take to save for the basketball hoop?

   Ⓐ $75 \div [(15 - 6) + (10 - 4)]$
   Ⓑ $75 \div [(15 + 6) - (10 - 4)]$
   Ⓒ $75 \div [(15 - 6) + (10 + 4)]$
   Ⓓ $75 \div [(15 - 6) - (10 - 4)]$

2. A hotel costs $89 per night. Sally will receive a $5 per night discount for paying in advance. A rental car costs $35 per day plus taxes that total $4 per day. Which expression can Sally use to find how much she will pay for the hotel and rental car for 5 days?

   Ⓐ $5 \times (89 - 5) - (35 + 4)$
   Ⓑ $[5 \times (89 - 5)] + (35 + 4)$
   Ⓒ $5 \times [(89 - 5) - (35 + 4)]$
   Ⓓ $5 \times [(89 - 5) + (35 + 4)]$

3. Of the 90 trading cards Yoshi has, 55 are baseball cards and 35 are football cards. He gives Henry 10 football cards and Henry gives Yoshi 8 baseball cards. Which expression can be used to find the number of trading cards Yoshi has now?

   Ⓐ $(55 + 8) - (35 + 10)$
   Ⓑ $(55 - 8) - (35 + 10)$
   Ⓒ $(55 - 8) + (35 - 10)$
   Ⓓ $(55 + 8) + (35 - 10)$

4. Jonah is a baker. Each morning, he makes 60 cupcakes. He gives away 5 and sells the rest. Each morning, he also makes 48 brownies. He gives away 4 and sells the rest. Which expression can be used to find how many cupcakes and brownies Jonah sells in 7 days?

   Ⓐ $7 \times [(60 - 5) - (48 - 4)]$
   Ⓑ $7 \times [(60 - 5) + (48 - 4)]$
   Ⓒ $[7 \times (60 - 5)] + (48 - 4)$
   Ⓓ $7 \times (60 - 5) + (48 - 4)$

5. Evaluate the expression $2 \times [(25 + 3) + (15 - 2)]$. Explain your work.

   Possible explanation: Simplify the expression in the first set of parentheses: $25 + 3 = 28$. Then, simplify the expression in the second set of parentheses: $15 - 2 = 13$. Next, simplify the expression in the brackets: $28 + 13 = 41$. Finally, multiply: $2 \times 41 = 82$.

2   **Operations and Algebraic Thinking**

Name _____

Lesson 3
CC.5.OA.2

1. Jamie baked 24 cupcakes. Her sister Mia ate 3 cupcakes, and her brother David ate 2 cupcakes. Which expression can Jamie use to find how many cupcakes are left?

   Ⓐ $24 + (3 - 2)$
   Ⓑ $24 - (3 + 2)$
   Ⓒ $(24 - 3) + 2$
   Ⓓ $24 - (3 - 2)$

2. Paul displays his sports trophies on shelves in his room. He has 5 trophies on each of 3 shelves and 2 trophies on another shelf. Which expression could Paul use to find the total number of trophies displayed?

   Ⓐ $(5 \times 3) - 2$
   Ⓑ $5 \times (3 + 2)$
   Ⓒ $5 + (3 \times 2)$
   Ⓓ $(5 \times 3) + 2$

3. William won 50 tickets at the arcade. He redeemed 30 tickets for a prize and gave 5 tickets to Katelyn. Which expression can William use to find how many tickets he has left?

   Ⓐ $50 - (30 + 5)$
   Ⓑ $50 + (30 - 5)$
   Ⓒ $(50 + 30) + 5$
   Ⓓ $50 - (30 - 5)$

4. Rupal poured muffin batter into 3 muffin tins. Each muffin tin holds 8 muffins. She kept 6 muffins and took the rest to school for the bake sale. Which expression could be used to find the total number of muffins Rupal took to school for the bake sale?

   Ⓐ $(3 \times 8) + 6$
   Ⓑ $(3 + 8) - 6$
   Ⓒ $(3 \times 8) - 6$
   Ⓓ $3 \times (8 - 6)$

5. There are 12 apartments on each floor of a building. All but 3 apartments on each floor have one bedroom. The building has 4 floors. Explain how you could write an expression to find the number of one-bedroom apartments in the building.

   Possible explanation: I could multiply the number of one-bedroom apartments on each floor by the number of floors. The number of one-bedroom apartments on each floor is $(12 - 3)$. So the expression would be $4 \times (12 - 3)$.

Operations and Algebraic Thinking   3

Name _____

Lesson 4
CC.5.OA.3

Use the table for 1–2.

Jawan made a table to figure out how much he earns at his job.

Job Earnings

Days	1	2	3	4
Hours Worked	6	12	18	24
Amount Earned ($)	54	108	162	216

1. What rule relates the hours worked to the amount earned?

   Ⓐ Add 6.
   Ⓑ Add 54.
   Ⓒ Multiply by 2.
   Ⓓ Multiply by 9.

2. Suppose Jawan works 6 days. Using the rule that relates the hours worked to the amount earned, find the total number of hours he will work in 6 days and how much money he will earn in all.

   Ⓐ 36 hours, $648
   Ⓑ 36 hours, $324
   Ⓒ 30 hours, $300
   Ⓓ 30 hours, $270

3. What is the unknown number in Sequence 2 in the chart?

Sequence Number	1	2	3	5	7
Sequence 1	3	6	9	15	21
Sequence 2	15	30	45	75	?

   Ⓐ 63
   Ⓑ 90
   Ⓒ 105
   Ⓓ 150

4. Wanda made a table to show the number of ounces of flour she uses to make cupcakes.

   Flour in Cupcakes

Batches	1	2	3	4	6
Ounces of Flour	8	16	24	32	48
Cupcakes	16	32	48	64	96

   What rule relates the number of ounces of flour to the number of cupcakes?

   Ⓐ Add 8.
   Ⓑ Add 12.
   Ⓒ Multiply by 2.
   Ⓓ Multiply by 8.

5. Mrs. Marston determined how many tubes of paint she would need for the students in her art classes to complete their projects. How many tubes of paint will she need for the class with 20 students? Explain how you found the answer.

Students	4	8	12	16	20
Tubes	8	16	24	32	40

   40 tubes of paint; I could see that a rule is multiply the number of students by 2 to find the number of tubes; $20 \times 2 = 40$.

4   **Operations and Algebraic Thinking**

© Houghton Mifflin Harcourt Publishing Company

Answer Key

101

1. Nomi is making a pattern of square tiles, as shown below. The side lengths of the tiles are 2 centimeters.

2 cm [square with sides labeled 2 cm, 2 cm, 2 cm, 2 cm] 2 cm

Figure 1   Figure 2   Figure 3

Suppose Nomi continues the pattern. What will be the distance around Figure 7?

Ⓐ 14 centimeters
Ⓑ 49 centimeters
Ⓒ 56 centimeters
Ⓓ 98 centimeters

2. Leroy starts to work at a part-time job. He saves $25 of his earnings each month. By the end of the second month, he saves $50 in all. How much will he save by the end of 24 months?

Ⓐ $75   Ⓒ $1,200
Ⓑ $600   Ⓓ $1,800

Use the table for 3–4.

The table shows the number of tickets needed for rides at an amusement park.

Amusement Park Rides

Number of Rides	1	2	3	7
Number of Tickets	4	8	12	?

3. Which rule relates the number of tickets to the number of rides?

Ⓐ Multiply the number of rides by 4.
Ⓑ Multiply the number of rides by 3.
Ⓒ Add 3 for each ride.
Ⓓ Add 4 for each ride.

4. Jared buys 40 tickets and goes on 7 rides. How many tickets does he have left after the 7 rides?

Ⓐ 33   Ⓒ 24
Ⓑ 28   **Ⓓ 12**

5. A restaurant manager has 10 tables that are 3 feet wide and 4 feet long. Suppose the manager places the 10 tables side-by-side so the 4-foot sides match up. What will be the perimeter of the larger table that is formed? Explain how you know.

3 ft
4 ft

The perimeter of the larger table will be 68 feet. I know because the perimeter of 1 small table is 14 feet. Each time a small table is added, 6 feet is added to the perimeter. With 9 small tables added, that would be 9 × 6 or 54 feet added. So the perimeter of the larger table is

14 + 54 = 68 feet.

Use the graph for 1–3.

The graph shows the relationship between the time and the number of push ups Eric did.

[graph: Number of Push-Ups vs Time (minutes)]

1. What is the total number of push ups Eric did in 3 minutes?

Ⓐ 40   Ⓒ 50
Ⓑ 45   Ⓓ 55

2. What rule relates the number of push ups to the time?

Ⓐ Multiply the number of minutes by $\frac{1}{15}$.
Ⓑ Multiply the number of minutes by $\frac{1}{10}$.
Ⓒ Multiply the number of minutes by 10.
Ⓓ Multiply the number of minutes by 15.

3. Suppose Eric continues to do push ups at this rate. What is the total number of push ups he will do in 5 minutes?

Ⓐ 50   Ⓒ 75
Ⓑ 65   **Ⓓ 90**

4. Randy makes a table that shows how long it takes her to run different distances.

Running Time and Distance

Number of miles	1	2	3	4
Time (in minutes)	10	20	30	40

Draw a line graph to show the relationship between the number of miles and the time. Explain how you can use the graph to find how long it will take Randy to run 5 miles at the same rate.

[graph: Time (in minutes) vs Number of Miles]

It will take Randy 50 minutes to run 5 miles. I know because the line on my graph goes through (5, 50). The 5 in the ordered pair stands for 5 miles, and the 50 stands for 50 minutes.

1. A math workbook contains 50 pages. The number of problems in the book is 10 times as many as the number of pages. How many problems are in the math workbook?

Ⓐ 5
Ⓑ 500
Ⓒ 5,000
Ⓓ 50,000

2. Cara has saved $4,000 to buy a car. Rick wants to buy a new television set. He has saved $\frac{1}{10}$ as much as Cara. How much has Rick saved?

Ⓐ $4
Ⓑ $40
Ⓒ $400
Ⓓ $40,000

3. Riva lives 300 miles from her grandparents. George lives 10 times that distance from his grandparents. How many miles does George live from his grandparents?

Ⓐ 30
Ⓑ 3,000
Ⓒ 30,000
Ⓓ 300,000

4. The Davis family pays $200,000 for a new house. They make a down payment that is $\frac{1}{10}$ of the price of the house. How much is the down payment?

Ⓐ $20
Ⓑ $200
Ⓒ $2,000
Ⓓ $20,000

5. Joshua earns $60,000 a year at his job. He is getting a raise that is $\frac{1}{10}$ of the amount he earns now. Joshua says that his new salary will be $60,600. Do you agree? Support your answer.

No; Possible answer: Joshua's raise will be $\frac{1}{10}$ of $60,000, or $6,000. His new salary will be $60,000 + $6,000, or $66,000.

1. A publisher reports that it sold 2,419,386 children's magazines. What is the value of the digit 2 in 2,419,386?

Ⓐ 200,000,000
Ⓑ 20,000,000
Ⓒ 2,000,000
Ⓓ 200,000

2. The diameter of Saturn at its equator is about 120,540,000 meters. What is 120,540,000 written in word form?

Ⓐ twelve thousand, five hundred forty
Ⓑ twelve million, five hundred forty thousand
Ⓒ one hundred twenty million, fifty-four thousand
Ⓓ one hundred twenty million, five hundred forty thousand

3. A printing company used 1,896,432 sheets of tag board last year. What is the value of the digit 8 in 1,896,432?

Ⓐ 800
Ⓑ 8,000
Ⓒ 80,000
Ⓓ 800,000

4. A company manufactured forty-eight million, seven hundred fifty thousand toothpicks last month. What is this number written in standard form?

Ⓐ 48,750,000
Ⓑ 48,700,050
Ⓒ 48,000,750
Ⓓ 48,750

5. Rayna lives in Fulton, which has a population of 260,980 people. Rayna wrote 260,980 as (2 × 100,000) + (6 × 10,000) + (9 × 1,000) + (8 × 100). What error did Rayna make? Write the correct expanded form.

Possible answer: Rayna did not use the correct place values in the expanded form for the numbers in the hundreds and tens places. The correct expanded form is (2 × 100,000) + (6 × 10,000) + (9 × 100) + (8 × 10).

Lesson 9
CC.5.NBT.1

1. A calculator is 0.07 meter wide. Sam made a model that was $\frac{1}{10}$ the size of the actual calculator. How wide was Sam's model?

   (A) 70 meters
   (B) 7 meters
   (C) 0.7 meter
   (D) 0.007 meter

2. A word in a book is 0.009 meter long. Kai looked at the word with a lens that made it look 10 times as large as the actual word. How long did the word look?

   (A) 0.0009 meter
   (B) 0.09 meter
   (C) 0.9 meter
   (D) 9 meters

3. What is the relationship between 0.008 and 0.08?

   (A) 0.008 is $\frac{1}{10}$ of 0.08.
   (B) 0.08 is $\frac{1}{10}$ of 0.008.
   (C) 0.008 is 10 times as much as 0.08.
   (D) 0.008 is equal to 0.08.

4. Valerie made a model for a decimal. What decimal is shown by Valerie's model?

   (A) 0.026   (C) 0.216
   (B) 0.206   (D) 0.26

5. A jeweler used 0.5 ounce of gold to make a necklace. He used $\frac{1}{10}$ as much gold in an earring. Explain how to use place-value patterns to find how much gold the jeweler used in the earring.

   Possible explanation: each place value is $\frac{1}{10}$ of the place value to its left. The decimal 0.5 is in tenths, so the decimal for $\frac{1}{10}$ of 0.5 would be in hundredths, or 0.05.

Lesson 10
CC.5.NBT.2

1. A Coast Guard ship is responsible for searching an area that is 5,000 square miles. Which shows 5,000 as a whole number multiplied by a power of ten?

   (A) 5×10^1
   (B) 5×10^2
   (C) 5×10^3
   (D) 5×10^4

2. Martin is going mountain climbing at Snowmass Mountain in Colorado. He looked up the height of the mountain and found it to be about 14×10^3 feet high. What is the height of Snowmass Mountain written as a whole number?

   (A) 140 feet
   (B) 1,400 feet
   (C) 14,000 feet
   (D) 140,000 feet

3. Patel hopes to be one of the first fans to get into the stadium for the baseball game because the first 30,000 fans will receive a baseball cap. Which shows 30,000 as a whole number multiplied by a power of ten?

   (A) 3×10^1
   (B) 3×10^2
   (C) 3×10^3
   (D) 3×10^4

4. Trisha is writing a report about Guam for Social Studies. She looked up the population of Guam and found it to be about 18×10^4. What is the population of Guam written as a whole number?

   (A) 180,000
   (B) 18,000
   (C) 1,800
   (D) 180

5. June wrote an essay on saving energy for a contest. She won a $5,000 scholarship. Explain how June can write $5,000 as a whole number multiplied by a power of ten in two different ways.

   Possible explanation: June can write 5,000 as 5×10^3 since $5,000 = 5 \times 1,000$ and $1,000 = 10^3$. She can also write 5,000 as 50×10^2 since $5,000 = 50 \times 100$ and $100 = 10^2$.

Lesson 11
CC.5.NBT.2

1. A country music concert will be held at a local park. The promoters have already sold 3,000 concert tickets. Each ticket costs $20. How much money have the promoters already collected?

   (A) $60
   (B) $600
   (C) $60,000
   (D) $600,000

2. Clinton decided to buy 300 shares of stock in an electronics company. Each share costs $60. Which of the following could he use to find the total amount he will pay for the stock?

   (A) $(6 \times 3) \times 10^2 = 1,800$
   (B) $(6 \times 3) \times 10^3 = 18,000$
   (C) $(6 \times 3) \times 10^4 = 180,000$
   (D) $(6 \times 3) \times 10^5 = 1,800,000$

3. Sam is using a microscope to look at a plant specimen. The microscope magnifies the specimen 4×10^2 times. If the specimen is 3 centimeters long, how long will the magnified specimen appear to be?

   (A) 70 centimeters
   (B) 120 centimeters
   (C) 700 centimeters
   (D) 1,200 centimeters

4. So far the fifth-grade students at Silver Run Elementary School have raised $200 toward their class trip. They need to raise 8 times as much to pay for the whole trip. How much money do the fifth-grade students need to raise in all?

   (A) $16
   (B) $1,600
   (C) $16,000
   (D) $160,000

5. The Yukon River in British Columbia is about 4 times as long as the Osage River in Kansas. If the Osage River is 5×10^2 miles long, about how long is the Yukon River? Explain how you found your answer.

   2,000 miles; Possible explanation: I multiplied $4 \times (5 \times 10^2)$. I used the Associative Property of Multiplication to regroup the factors as $(4 \times 5) \times 10^2$ which is 20×100, or 2,000.

Lesson 12
CC.5.NBT.2

1. Ganesh is making a scale model of the Space Needle in Seattle, Washington, for a report on the state of Washington. The Space Needle is 605 feet tall. If the model is $\frac{1}{100}$ of the actual size of the Space Needle, how tall is the model?

   (A) 0.605 foot
   (B) 6.05 feet
   (C) 6.5 feet
   (D) 60.5 feet

2. Madison needs to buy enough meat to make 1,000 hamburgers for the company picnic. Each hamburger will weigh 0.25 pound. How many pounds of hamburger meat should Madison buy?

   (A) 2.5 pounds
   (B) 25 pounds
   (C) 250 pounds
   (D) 2,500 pounds

3. Kareem was doing research for a report about the longest rivers on Earth. He read that the Nile River is 4.16×10^3 miles long. How should Kareem write the length of the Nile River in standard form on his report?

   (A) 4.16 miles
   (B) 41.6 miles
   (C) 416 miles
   (D) 4,160 miles

4. The school store expects to sell a lot of sweatshirts because the football team won the championship. The store ordered 100 sweatshirts. Each sweatshirt cost $8.95. How much did the order of sweatshirts cost the store?

   (A) $89.50
   (B) $895
   (C) $8,950
   (D) $89,500

5. Nathan put 0.35 quart of concentrated liquid cleaner in a bucket. Then he put 10 times that amount of water in the bucket. Nathan says he added 35 quarts of water to the bucket. Do you agree? Support your answer.

   I disagree; Possible answer: I wrote a pattern to find the amount of water: $1 \times 0.35 = 0.35$, $10 \times 0.35 = 3.5$. So, Nathan put 3.5 quarts of water into the bucket, not 35 quarts.

Answer Key

Lesson 13
CC.5.NBT.2

1. Lori is running in a marathon, which is 26.2 miles long. So far, she has run one-tenth of the marathon. How far has Lori run?

   Ⓐ 262 miles

   Ⓑ 2.62 miles

   Ⓒ 0.262 mile

   Ⓓ 0.00262 mile

2. A school bought 1,000 erasers as part of an order for supplies. The total cost of the erasers was $30. What was the cost of 1 eraser?

   Ⓐ $0.03

   Ⓑ $0.30

   Ⓒ $300

   Ⓓ $3,000

3. Tanya baked 100 cupcakes one morning in a bakery. She used 64 ounces of frosting to decorate the cupcakes. If each cupcake had the same amount of frosting, how much frosting did Tanya put on each cupcake?

   Ⓐ 0.0064 ounce

   Ⓑ 0.064 ounce

   Ⓒ 0.64 ounce

   Ⓓ 6.4 ounces

4. A counselor at Sleepy Hollow Camp has 225 yards of lanyard to give to 100 campers to make lanyard key chains. Each camper will get the same amount of lanyard. How much lanyard will each camper get?

   Ⓐ 0.0225 yard

   Ⓑ 0.225 yard

   Ⓒ 2.25 yards

   Ⓓ 22.5 yards

5. Thomas paid $50 for a box of multicolor file folders for his office. There were 100 folders in the box. He said that the cost of each folder was $0.05. Do you agree? Support your answer.

   No; Possible answer: the cost of a folder is $0.50. I used

   a pattern to divide 50 by 100. The pattern is:

   $50 ÷ 1 = $50; $50 ÷ 10 = $5; $50 ÷ 100 = $0.5,

   or $0.50.

Lesson 14
CC.5.NBT.3a

1. A scientist measured a grain of sand. It had a diameter of 0.049 millimeter. What is 0.049 written in word form?

   Ⓐ forty-nine

   Ⓑ forty-nine tenths

   Ⓒ forty-nine hundredths

   Ⓓ forty-nine thousandths

2. The diamond in Alma's necklace weighs 0.258 carat. What digit is in the hundredths place of 0.258?

   Ⓐ 0

   Ⓑ 2

   Ⓒ 5

   Ⓓ 8

3. The mass of an ant is about 0.003 gram. What is the value of the digit 3 in 0.003?

   Ⓐ 3 ones

   Ⓑ 3 tenths

   Ⓒ 3 hundredths

   Ⓓ 3 thousandths

4. A penny has a diameter of 0.019 meter. What is 0.019 written in word form?

   Ⓐ nineteen thousandths

   Ⓑ nineteen hundredths

   Ⓒ nineteen tenths

   Ⓓ nineteen

5. Zeke wrote the number six and fifty-eight thousandths as 6.58. Describe Zeke's error and tell how you would correct it.

   Possible answer: Zeke did not include a place holder in

   the tenths place. The correct answer is 6.058.

Lesson 15
CC.5.NBT.3b

1. Harry kept a record of how far he ran each day last week.

Day	Distance (in miles)
Monday	4.5
Tuesday	3.9
Wednesday	4.25
Thursday	3.75
Friday	4.2

On which day did Harry run the greatest number of miles?

   Ⓐ Monday

   Ⓑ Tuesday

   Ⓒ Thursday

   Ⓓ Friday

2. The four highest scores on the floor exercise at a gymnastics meet were 9.675, 9.25, 9.325, and 9.5. Which shows the order of the scores from least to greatest?

   Ⓐ 9.5, 9.25, 9.325, 9.675

   Ⓑ 9.25, 9.5, 9.325, 9.675

   Ⓒ 9.675, 9.5, 9.325, 9.25

   Ⓓ 9.25, 9.325, 9.5, 9.675

3. The table shows the fastest times for the 100-meter hurdles event.

Name	Times (in seconds)
Shakira	15.45
Jameel	15.09
Lindsay	15.6
Nicholas	15.3

Who had the fastest time?

   Ⓐ Shakira   Ⓒ Lindsay

   Ⓑ Jameel   Ⓓ Nicholas

4. Mary Ann kept a record of how long she practiced the piano each week for a month.

Week	Hours Practiced
Week 1	4.75
Week 2	4.5
Week 3	5.1
Week 4	5.75

During which week did Mary Ann practice the greatest amount of time?

   Ⓐ Week 1   Ⓒ Week 3

   Ⓑ Week 2   Ⓓ Week 4

5. In a balance beam event, Eva scored 9.375 points and Yuko scored 9.325 points. How should Eva and Yuko compare their scores to find who had the greater score? Explain your answer.

   hundredths place; Possible explanation: they need to

   compare ones and tenths to find out they are the same.

   The scores differ in the hundredths place: 7 > 2,

   so 9.375 > 9.325.

Lesson 16
CC.5.NBT.4

1. It takes the dwarf planet Pluto 247.68 years to revolve once around the sun. What is 247.68 years rounded to the nearest whole number of years?

   Ⓐ 247 years

   Ⓑ 247.6 years

   Ⓒ 247.7 years

   Ⓓ 248 years

2. The flagpole in front of Silver Pines Elementary School is 18.375 feet tall. What is 18.375 rounded to the nearest tenth?

   Ⓐ 18

   Ⓑ 18.38

   Ⓒ 18.4

   Ⓓ 20

3. Michelle records the value of one Euro in U.S. dollars each day for her social studies project. The table shows the data she has recorded so far.

Day	Value of 1 Euro (In U.S. dollars)
Monday	1.448
Tuesday	1.443
Wednesday	1.452
Thursday	1.458

On which day does the value of 1 Euro round to $1.46 to the nearest hundredth?

   Ⓐ Monday   Ⓒ Wednesday

   Ⓑ Tuesday   Ⓓ Thursday

4. Jackie found a rock that has a mass of 78.852 grams. What is the mass of the rock rounded to the nearest tenth?

   Ⓐ 78.85 grams   Ⓒ 79 grams

   Ⓑ 78.9 grams   Ⓓ 80 grams

5. It takes the planet Neptune about 164.8 years to revolve once around the sun. What are the least and greatest numbers written in hundredths that could round to 164.8? Explain your answer.

   Possible answer: The least number is 164.75. Any lesser

   number would round to 164.7. The greatest number is

   164.84. Any greater number would round to 164.9.

Answer Key

1. A bus driver travels 234 miles every day. How many miles does the bus driver travel in 5 days?
   - (A) 1,050 miles
   - (B) 1,150 miles
   - (C) 1,170 miles
   - (D) 1,520 miles

2. Hector does 165 sit-ups every day. How many sit-ups does he do in 7 days?
   - (A) 1,155
   - (B) 1,145
   - (C) 1,125
   - (D) 725

3. Lara and Chad are both saving to buy cars. So far, Chad has saved $1,235. Lara has saved 5 times as much as Chad. How much has Lara saved?
   - (A) $5,055
   - (B) $6,055
   - (C) $6,075
   - (D) $6,175

4. Mavis drives 634 miles to visit her grandmother in Philadelphia. How many miles does Mavis drive if she visits her grandmother 4 times?
   - (A) 2,426 miles
   - (B) 2,436 miles
   - (C) 2,536 miles
   - (D) 2,836 miles

5. Cheryl and Richard decided to spend 5 months a year in Florida. The rent for the apartment they like is $885 per month. Cheryl said the total rent would be $40,425. Richard said the total rent would be $4,425. Explain how you can use an estimate to determine who is correct.

   Possible explanation: I can use 900 × 5 to estimate the product. My estimate would be $4,500. Since the rounded number of 900 is 15 more than the cost of the apartment, I can multiply 15 × 5 and get $75. Since $4,425 is $75 less than the estimate of $4,500, I can conclude that Richard must be correct.

1. Chen burns 354 calories in 1 hour swimming. He swam for 28 hours last month. How many calories did Chen burn in all last month from swimming?
   - (A) 3,010 calories
   - (B) 8,482 calories
   - (C) 9,912 calories
   - (D) 10,266 calories

2. Rachel earns $27 per hour at work. She worked 936 hours last year. How much did Rachel earn working last year?
   - (A) $7,584
   - (B) $24,932
   - (C) $25,272
   - (D) $25,332

3. A company manufactures 295 toy cars each day. How many toy cars do they manufacture in 34 days?
   - (A) 3,065
   - (B) 7,610
   - (C) 10,065
   - (D) 10,030

4. Raul earns $24 per hour painting houses. If he works for 263 hours, how much will Raul earn in all?
   - (A) $6,312
   - (B) $6,112
   - (C) $5,102
   - (D) $1,578

5. Last year, Danielle worked 35 hours a week in a bookstore and earned $11 an hour. Danielle says that she earned about $20,000 last year. Do you agree? Support your answer with information from the problem.

   Yes; Possible answer: Danielle earned $385 per week: 35 × $11 = $385. There are 52 weeks in a year, so I estimated 52 × $385. I rounded 52 to the nearest ten, which is 50, and 385 to the nearest hundred dollars, which is $400. 50 × $400 = $20,000.

1. Sherry's family is going to a beach resort. Sherry bought 7 beach towels that cost $13 each to take to the resort. To find the total cost, she added the products of 7 × 10 and 7 × 3, for a total of $91. What property did Sherry use?
   - (A) Commutative Property of Multiplication
   - (B) Commutative Property of Addition
   - (C) Associative Property of Multiplication
   - (D) Distributive Property

2. Chen bought a basketball for $23, a pair of running shoes for $35, and a baseball cap for $7. He wrote the equation 23 + 35 + 7 = 23 + 7 + 35. What property did Chen use?
   - (A) Associative Property of Addition
   - (B) Commutative Property of Addition
   - (C) Distributive Property
   - (D) Identity Property of Multiplication

3. Nicole baked 9 trays of cookies. Each tray had 5 rows with 4 cookies in each row. Nicole wrote the equation (9 × 5) × 4 = 9 × (5 × 4). What property did Nicole use?
   - (A) Commutative Property of Multiplication
   - (B) Associative Property of Addition
   - (C) Associative Property of Multiplication
   - (D) Distributive Property

4. Ramon has a large collection of marbles. He has 150 clear marbles, 214 blue marbles, and 89 green marbles. Ramon wrote this equation about his marble collection:

   (150 + 214) + 89 = 150 + (214 + 89)

   What property did Ramon use?
   - (A) Associative Property of Addition
   - (B) Commutative Property of Addition
   - (C) Identity Property of Addition
   - (D) Distributive Property

5. Allison and Justin's father donated $3 for every lap they swam in a swim-a-thon. Allison swam 21 laps and Justin swam 15 laps. Use the Distributive Property to find the amount of money their father donated.

   Possible answer: the Distributive Property says that 3 × (21 + 15) = (3 × 21) + (3 × 15) = 63 + 45 = 108. He donated $108.

1. Francine took 42 photos with her digital camera. She stored an equal number of photos in each of 3 folders on her computer. Which multiplication sentence could Francine use to find the number of photos in each folder?
   - (A) 3 × 14 = 42
   - (B) 3 × 40 = 120
   - (C) 3 × 42 = 126
   - (D) 4 × 42 = 168

2. Amber baked 120 cookies to give to 5 friends. She wants to put the same number of cookies in each bag. Which of the following can she use to find how many cookies to put in each bag?
   - (A) (5 × 20) + (5 × 4)
   - (B) (5 × 10) + (5 × 8)
   - (C) (5 × 60) + (5 × 2)
   - (D) (5 × 15) + (5 × 5)

3. Shari sent a total of 64 text messages to 4 friends. Each friend received the same number of text messages. Which multiplication sentence could Shari use to find the number of text messages she sent to each friend?
   - (A) 4 × 64 = 256
   - (B) 60 × 4 = 240
   - (C) 5 × 64 = 320
   - (D) 4 × 16 = 64

4. Jared has 96 books to arrange on 6 shelves of a bookcase. He wants each shelf to have the same number of books. Which of the following cannot be used to find how many books Jared can put on each shelf?
   - (A) (6 × 10) + (6 × 6)
   - (B) (6 × 8) + (6 × 8)
   - (C) (6 × 4) + (6 × 4)
   - (D) (6 × 15) + (6 × 1)

5. Lee has 72 photos to put into a photo album. He can put 3 photos on each page. Explain how Lee can use the Distributive Property to divide and find the number of pages he will use in the album.

   Possible explanation: Lee can write 3 × ? = 72, which is the related multiplication sentence for 72 ÷ 3 = ?. Then he can use the Distributive Property to break apart the product: (3 × 20) + (3 × 4) = 72. The sum of 20 and 4 is the missing factor, 24. So Lee will use 24 pages in the photo album.

Answer Key

1. Marta has 16 postcards from each of 8 different cities in Pennsylvania. She can fit 4 postcards on each page of her scrapbook. How many pages in the scrapbook can Marta fill with postcards?

   Ⓐ 32
   Ⓑ 41
   Ⓒ 128
   Ⓓ 512

2. Nathan's orchestra has 18 string musicians, 9 percussion musicians, 15 brass musicians, and 12 woodwind musicians. Six of the musicians cannot play in the next performance. If the remaining musicians plan to sit in rows of 6 chairs, how many rows of chairs are needed?

   Ⓐ 4
   Ⓑ 6
   Ⓒ 8
   Ⓓ 9

3. There are 6 buses transporting students to a baseball game, with 32 students on each bus. Each row at the baseball stadium seats 8 students. If the students fill up all of the rows, how many rows of seats will the students need altogether?

   Ⓐ 22
   Ⓑ 23
   Ⓒ 24
   Ⓓ 1,536

4. Laura has 24 stamps from each of 6 different countries. She can fit 4 stamps on each display sheet of an album. How many display sheets can Laura fill with stamps?

   Ⓐ 576
   Ⓑ 36
   Ⓒ 34
   Ⓓ 16

5. Ming's DVD collection includes 16 adventure movies, 7 comedies, 12 westerns, and 8 mysteries. He wants to keep 2 of each type of DVD and give away the rest. Ming says that if he gives an equal number of DVDs to 5 friends, he will give each friend 7 DVDs. Do you agree? Support your answer.

   Yes; Possible explanation: I added 16 + 7 + 12 + 8 = 43 to find how many DVDs Ming has. Since Ming wants to keep 2 of each of 4 types, I multiplied 2 × 4 = 8 DVDs Ming will keep. So, Ming will give away 43 − 8, = 35 DVDs to 5 friends. I divided 35 by 5 to find how many DVDs each friend will get, which is 7.

1. Caleb needs to solve the problem 2,406 ÷ 6. In what place is the first digit of the quotient for the problem 2,406 ÷ 6?

   Ⓐ ones
   Ⓑ tens
   Ⓒ hundreds
   Ⓓ thousands

2. Mrs. Tao has 154 books on 7 shelves in her classroom. Each shelf has the same number of books on it. She wants to find out the number of books on each shelf. In what place should Mrs. Tao write the first digit of the quotient for the problem 154 ÷ 7?

   Ⓐ ones
   Ⓑ tens
   Ⓒ hundreds
   Ⓓ thousands

3. The last problem on Jacob's math test was 9,072 ÷ 9. In what place should Jacob write the first digit of the quotient for the problem 9,072 ÷ 9?

   Ⓐ ones
   Ⓑ tens
   Ⓒ hundreds
   Ⓓ thousands

4. Raul has 486 baseball cards in 9 albums. Each album has the same number of baseball cards. He wants to find the number of baseball cards in each album. In what place should Raul write the first digit of the quotient for the problem 486 ÷ 9?

   Ⓐ ones
   Ⓑ tens
   Ⓒ hundreds
   Ⓓ thousands

5. Elizabeth was assigned the problem 3,402 ÷ 6 for homework. Explain how Elizabeth could use place value to write the first digit in the quotient of 3,402 ÷ 6.

   Possible answer: Elizabeth could look at the thousands and reason that 3 thousands cannot be shared among 6 groups without regrouping. 34 hundreds can be shared among 6 groups, so the first digit in the quotient is in the hundreds place.

1. During a school fund raiser, the fifth-grade classes sold rolls of wrapping paper. The table shows how many rolls each class sold. The rolls were sold in packages of 4.

   Wrapping Paper Sold

Class	Total Rolls
Ms. Lane	672
Mr. Milner	184
Mrs. Jackson	228

   How many packages of wrapping paper did Ms. Lane's class sell?

   Ⓐ 2,688
   Ⓑ 173
   Ⓒ 168
   Ⓓ 143

2. Sophia wants to buy collector boxes that can hold 6 dolls each. How many boxes will Sophia need to buy for her collection of 168 dolls?

   Ⓐ 21
   Ⓑ 28
   Ⓒ 34
   Ⓓ 1,008

3. On a standard week-long space shuttle flight, 175 servings of fresh food are shared equally among 7 crewmembers. How many servings of fresh food does each crewmember receive?

   Ⓐ 25
   Ⓑ 26
   Ⓒ 32
   Ⓓ 33

4. A bakery sold croissants to local restaurants. The table shows how many croissants were sold to each restaurant. The croissants were sold 6 to a box.

   Croissants Sold

Restaurant	Number of Croissants
The Coffee Counter	546
La Claudette	768
Bon Jour	858

   How many boxes of croissants did the bakery sell to La Claudette?

   Ⓐ 4,608
   Ⓑ 143
   Ⓒ 128
   Ⓓ 96

5. Avery made mosaic tile trays for a craft fair. He used 4,072 tiles to make 8 trays. Each tray had the same number of tiles. Avery made a display saying that he used 59 tiles for each tray. Was Avery's sign correct? Support your answer with information from the problem.

   Possible answer: Avery's sign was not correct. I used compatible numbers to place the first digit in the hundreds place, not the tens place. 4,000 ÷ 8 = 500. Then I divided: 4,072 ÷ 8 = 509. My answer is reasonable because the estimate of 500 is close to 509.

1. Emma used a quick picture to help her divide 154 by 11. What is the quotient?

   Ⓐ 11
   Ⓑ 12
   Ⓒ 13
   Ⓓ 14

2. Garrett used a quick picture to help him divide 182 by 14. What is the quotient?

   Ⓐ 11
   Ⓑ 12
   Ⓒ 13
   Ⓓ 14

3. Latoya drew a quick picture to solve a division problem. Which division problem does the quick picture show?

   Ⓐ 195 ÷ 15 = 13
   Ⓑ 169 ÷ 13 = 13
   Ⓒ 180 ÷ 15 = 12
   Ⓓ 165 ÷ 15 = 11

4. Ling has 168 baseball cards. He put the same number of cards into each of 14 piles. How many baseball cards did Ling put in each pile?

   Ⓐ 11
   Ⓑ 12
   Ⓒ 13
   Ⓓ 14

5. Nick has 192 stickers. He buys a new sticker album and will put 16 stickers on each page of the album. Explain how Nick can use base-ten blocks to find how many full pages of stickers he will have.

   Possible answer: Nick can use the hundred block and 6 tens to make a rectangle with 10 groups of 16. Then he can combine the remaining 3 tens and 2 ones into 2 groups of 16. He can place those groups to the right of the rectangle to show 12 groups of 16.

1. Jacob divided 976 by 28 using partial quotients. What is missing from Jacob's work?

   34 r24
   28)976
   −280 ← 10 × 28   10
   ────
   696
   −280 ← 10 × 28   10
   ────
   416
   −280 ← 10 × 28   10
   ────
   136
   − □   ← 4 × 28   + 4
   ────   ────
   24   34

   Ⓐ 24   Ⓒ 112
   Ⓑ 34   Ⓓ 280

2. Orah takes an 18-day bike tour. She rides 756 miles in all. What is the average number of miles she rides each day?

   Ⓐ 32   Ⓒ 90
   Ⓑ 42   Ⓓ 92

3. Paloma divided 1,292 by 31 using partial quotients. What is the quotient?

   31)1,292
   −930 ← 30 × 31   30
   ────
   362
   −310 ← 10 × 31   10
   ────
   52
   −31   ← 1 × 31   + 1
   ────   ────
   21   41

   Ⓐ 21   Ⓒ 41
   Ⓑ 21 r41   **Ⓓ 41 r21**

4. The school library has 2,976 books on its shelves. Each shelf has 48 books on it. How many shelves are in the library?

   Ⓐ 42
   Ⓑ 52
   Ⓒ 62
   Ⓓ 192

5. Lainie has a collection of 1,824 stamps that she wants to put into envelopes. She wants to put 48 stamps into each envelope. How many envelopes does Lainie need? Describe the steps you would follow to find the answer using partial quotients with multiples of 20.

   38 envelopes; Possible answer: Since 48 × 20 = 960, I first subtract 960: 1,824 − 960 = 864. Then since 48 × 10 = 480, I subtract 480: 864 − 480 = 384. Then since 48 × 8 = 384, I get 384 − 384 = 0. Finally, I add the partial quotients to find the quotient: 20 + 10 + 8 = 38.

1. Lauren bought a television that cost $805. She plans to make equal payments of $38 each month until the television is paid in full. About how many payments will Lauren make?

   Ⓐ 20
   Ⓑ 30
   Ⓒ 38
   Ⓓ 40

2. Miss Roja plans to sell tote bags at the art festival for $33 each. She will need to make $265 to pay the rent for the space at the festival. About how many tote bags will she need to sell to pay the rent?

   Ⓐ 3
   Ⓑ 7
   Ⓒ 9
   Ⓓ 30

3. Mrs. Ortega bought a dishwasher that cost $579. She will make monthly payments in the amount of $28 until the dishwasher is paid in full. About how many payments will Mrs. Ortega make?

   Ⓐ 12
   Ⓑ 20
   Ⓒ 28
   Ⓓ 30

4. Doug plans to sell mugs at the craft fair for $21 each. He will need to make $182 to pay the rent for the space at the fair. About how many mugs will he need to sell to pay the rent?

   Ⓐ 2
   Ⓑ 6
   Ⓒ 9
   Ⓓ 20

5. Henry has 1,875 photos to put in albums which hold 72 photos each. He says he needs between 20 and 30 photo albums. Do you agree with Henry? Explain your answer using compatible numbers.

   Possible answer: I agree. I used compatible numbers to estimate 1,875 ÷ 72. I rounded the divisor to the nearest ten, which is 70, and found the multiples of 70 that 1,875 lie between. The multiples are 1,400 and 2,100. Then I used mental math to divide 1,400 ÷ 70 = 20 and 2,100 ÷ 70 = 30. Henry needs between 20 and 30 photo albums.

1. The local concert hall has 48 concerts scheduled this season. Each concert has the same number of tickets available for sale. There is a total of 4,560 tickets. How many tickets are available for each concert?

   Ⓐ 1,140
   Ⓑ 950
   Ⓒ 105
   Ⓓ 95

2. The director of a pet shelter received a shipment of 1,110 puppy blankets. He put the same number of blankets in each of 27 boxes and put the leftover blankets in the puppy kennels. How many blankets were put in the puppy kennels?

   Ⓐ 3
   Ⓑ 18
   Ⓒ 28
   Ⓓ 41

3. An airplane has 416 seats arranged in 52 rows. If there is the same number of seats in each row, how many seats are in one row?

   Ⓐ 21,632
   Ⓑ 364
   Ⓒ 8
   Ⓓ 6

4. Mr. Stephens needs to haul 1,518 tons of rock from a construction site. His dump truck can hold 26 tons per load. How many tons will Mr. Stephens need to haul in the last load to move all of the rock?

   Ⓐ 10
   Ⓑ 58
   Ⓒ 68
   Ⓓ 1,492

5. Meagan uses shipping boxes to mail 850 bags of glass beads. Each box can hold 24 bags. Meagan says there will be 10 bags of glass beads in the last box. Explain how Meagan could have reached that conclusion.

   Possible answer: Meagan divided 850, which is the total number of bags, by 24, which is the number of bags that each box can hold. 850 ÷ 24 = 35 r10. The answer tells her that she needs 36 boxes. There will be 24 bags in each of the first 35 boxes. The thirty-sixth box will have 10 bags in it because the remainder of 10 is the number of bags that she has to put into the last box.

1. To solve the division problem below, Kyle estimates that 2 is the first digit in the quotient.

   2
   29)556
   −58

   Which of the following is correct?

   Ⓐ 2 is the correct first digit of the quotient.
   Ⓑ 2 is too low. The first digit should be adjusted to 4.
   Ⓒ 2 is too low. The first digit should be adjusted to 3.
   Ⓓ 2 is too high. The first digit should be adjusted to 1.

2. Alex is saving up to buy a guitar that costs $855. He plans to save $45 a month. How many months will it take him to save enough money to buy the guitar?

   Ⓐ 19 months
   Ⓑ 21 months
   Ⓒ 23 months
   Ⓓ 25 months

3. An auditorium has 1,224 seats. There are 36 seats in each row. How many rows of seats are in the auditorium?

   Ⓐ 32
   Ⓑ 34
   Ⓒ 42
   Ⓓ 44

4. Diego estimates that 3 is the first digit in the quotient of the problem below.

   3
   16)4272
   −48

   Which of the following is correct?

   Ⓐ 3 is the correct first digit of the quotient.
   Ⓑ 3 is too low. The first digit should be adjusted to 4.
   Ⓒ 3 is too low. The first digit should be adjusted to 5.
   Ⓓ 3 is too high. The first digit should be adjusted to 2.

5. Carla is packing 768 baseball caps into boxes. She knows that 32 baseball caps will fit in each box. Carla divided the number of baseball caps by 32 to find the number of boxes she needs. She estimated and placed the first digit in the quotient.

   3
   32)768

   What is the next thing that Carla should do? Explain your answer.

   Possible answer: Carla must make a lower estimate because her estimate is too high. The product of the estimate and the divisor is 96, which is too large and cannot be subtracted.

Answer Key

Lesson 29
CC.5.NBT.6

1. Ricardo's dog weighs 6 times as much as his cat. The total weight of his two pets is 98 pounds. How much does Ricardo's dog weigh?

   (A) 92 pounds
   (B) 84 pounds
   (C) 16 pounds
   (D) 14 pounds

2. The number of children at the library was 3 times the number of adults. The total number of people at the library was 48. How many children were at the library?

   (A) 12
   (B) 24
   (C) 32
   (D) 36

3. Sarah baby-sat 7 times as many hours during summer break as she did during spring break. She baby-sat a total of 56 hours during both breaks. How many hours did Sarah baby-sit during spring break?

   (A) 49 hours
   (B) 9 hours
   (C) 8 hours
   (D) 7 hours

4. Melanie is 3 times as old as her cousin. The total of their ages is 36 years. How old is Melanie's cousin?

   (A) 9 years old
   (B) 12 years old
   (C) 27 years old
   (D) 33 years old

5. Ian and Joe took their younger sister Michelle to pick strawberries. Ian picked 5 times as many strawberries as Michelle. Joe picked 7 times as many strawberries as Michelle. Ian and Joe picked a total of 192 strawberries. How many strawberries did Joe pick? Use a diagram to help find the answer. Explain how you used the diagram to answer the question.

   <u>112 strawberries; Possible</u>
   <u>explanation: the total number</u>
   <u>of strawberries Ian and Joe</u>
   <u>picked are shown as 12 boxes.</u>
   <u>192 ÷ 12 = 16. This is the number</u>
   <u>that each box represents. So to</u>
   <u>find the number of strawberries</u>
   <u>that Joe picked, I multiplied 16 by 7.</u>

   Michelle's strawberries
   Ian's strawberries
   Joe's strawberries
   192 strawberries

Lesson 30
CC.5.NBT.7

1. Ken used a quick picture to model 1.77 + 1.19. Which picture shows the sum?

   (A)
   (B)
   (C)
   (D)

2. It took Margo 0.5 hour to do her science homework and 0.9 hour to do her math homework. How long did it take Margo to do her science and math homework?

   (A) 0.14 hour   (C) 1.04 hours
   (B) 0.45 hour   **(D) 1.4 hours**

3. It took Ray 0.45 hour to rake the leaves and 0.75 hour to mow the lawn. How long did it take Ray to rake the leaves and mow the lawn?

   (A) 0.12 hour   **(C) 1.2 hours**
   (B) 1.1 hours   (D) 1.21 hours

4. Hedy used decimal models to find the sum of 0.46 and 0.85. She drew a quick picture to represent the sum. Is Hedy correct? Explain your answer.

   <u>Yes; Possible explanation: 0.46 can be modeled with</u>
   <u>4 line segments to represent the tenths and 6 dots to</u>
   <u>represent the hundredths. 0.85 can be modeled with</u>
   <u>8 line segments to represent the tenths and 5 dots to</u>
   <u>represent the hundredths. Combine 10 tenths into</u>
   <u>1 one and 10 hundredths into 1 tenth. Then there will</u>
   <u>be 1 one, 3 tenths and 1 hundredth, which is what the</u>
   <u>model represents.</u>

Lesson 31
CC.5.NBT.7

1. Taryn used a quick picture to model 2.34 − 1.47. Which picture shows the difference?

   (A)
   (B)
   (C)
   (D)

2. Jasmine lives 1.25 miles from school and 0.82 mile from the library. How much farther does Jasmine live from school than from the library?

   (A) 0.33 mile   (C) 2.07 miles
   (B) 0.43 mile   (D) 4.3 miles

3. Avery bought 3.45 pounds of red apples and 1.57 pounds of green apples. How many more pounds of red apples than green apples did Avery buy?

   (A) 5.02 pounds
   (B) 1.98 pounds
   (C) 1.88 pounds
   (D) 1.12 pounds

4. Hector used decimal models to find 1.29 − 0.64. He drew a quick picture to represent the difference. Is Hector correct? Explain your answer.

   <u>No; Possible explanation: I can draw 1.29 using</u>
   <u>1 square for 1 one, 2 line segments for 2 tenths and</u>
   <u>9 dots for 9 hundredths. I can subtract 4 hundredths</u>
   <u>from 9 hundredths, leaving 5 hundredths. Next I would</u>
   <u>regroup 1 one as 10 tenths. Then I can subtract 6</u>
   <u>tenths from 12 tenths, which is 6 tenths. The difference</u>
   <u>is 0.65. Hector is incorrect because his quick picture</u>
   <u>shows 0.75.</u>

Lesson 32
CC.5.NBT.7

1. Julie has $16.73. She buys a purse that costs $4.12. About how much money will Julie have left?

   (A) $3
   (B) $13
   (C) $21
   (D) $23

2. A vet measured the mass of two birds. The mass of the robin was 76.64 grams. The mass of the blue jay was 81.54 grams. Which is the best estimate of the difference in the masses of the birds?

   (A) 5 grams
   (B) 10 grams
   (C) 15 grams
   (D) 20 grams

3. A town plans to add a 3.88-kilometer extension to a road that is currently 5.02 kilometers long. Which is the best estimate of the length of the road after the extension is added?

   (A) 1 kilometer
   (B) 2 kilometers
   (C) 4 kilometers
   (D) 9 kilometers

4. Denise has $78.22. She wants to buy a computer game that costs $29.99. About how much money will Denise have left?

   (A) $40
   (B) $50
   (C) $60
   (D) $110

5. Jennifer has $12 to spend on lunch and the roller rink. Admission to the roller rink is $5.75. Jennifer estimates that she can buy a large drink and a turkey sandwich, and still have enough money to get into the rink. Do you agree? Support your answer.

Sandwiches		Drinks	
Tuna	$3.95	Small	$1.29
Turkey	$4.85	Medium	$1.59
Grilled Cheese	$3.25	Large	$1.79

   <u>No; Possible answer: I rounded each amount to the</u>
   <u>nearest dollar. The admission to the roller rink is about</u>
   <u>$6, the large drink is about $2, and the turkey sandwich</u>
   <u>is about $5. $6 + $2 + $5 = $13, which is more than</u>
   <u>Jennifer has.</u>

Lesson 33
CC.5.NBT.7

1. Yolanda's sunflower plant was 64.34 centimeters tall in July. During August, the plant grew 58.7 centimeters. How tall was Yolanda's sunflower plant at the end of August?

   (A) 702.1 centimeters

   (B) 123.04 centimeters

   (C) 70.21 centimeters

   (**D**) 58.7 centimeters

2. Malcolm read that 2.75 inches of rain fell on Saturday. He read that 1.6 inches of rain fell on Sunday. How much rain fell on the two days?

   (A) 1.15 inches

   (B) 2.91 inches

   (C) 3.81 inches

   (**D**) 4.35 inches

3. Olivia bought a beach towel for $9.95 and a beach bag for $13.46. What is the total amount of money Olivia spent on the two items?.

   (A) $12.31

   (**B**) $23.41

   (C) $112.96

   (D) $144.55

4. Jon walked 1.75 kilometers on Monday and 3.2 kilometers on Wednesday. What was the total distance that Jon walked on Monday and Wednesday?

   (A) 33.75 kilometers

   (B) 20.7 kilometers

   (**C**) 4.95 kilometers

   (D) 2.07 kilometers

5. Gavin and Miles hiked 3.45 kilometers on Tuesday morning. After lunch they hiked another 6.5 kilometers. Gavin says they hiked 9.5 kilometers in all. Describe Gavin's error and correct it.

   Possible explanation: Gavin added the whole numbers 3 + 6 = 9 and the decimals 45 + 5 = 50 and wrote the sum as 9.50, or 9.5. Since 3.45 has hundredths and 6.5 does not, he should have written a zero to the right of the 5 in 6.5 to hold the hundredths place. Then, he should have added hundredths to hundredths, tenths to tenths, and ones to ones: 3.45 + 6.50 = 9.95. They hiked 9.95 kilometers in all.

Number and Operations in Base Ten   33

Lesson 34
CC.5.NBT.7

1. Juan had a 10.75-pound block of clay. He used 4.6 pounds of clay to make a sculpture of a horse. How much clay does Juan have left?

   (**A**) 6.1 pounds

   (B) 6.15 pounds

   (C) 10.29 pounds

   (D) 15.35 pounds

2. Ella and Nick are meeting at the library. The library is 4.61 kilometers from Ella's house and 3.25 kilometers from Nick's house. How much farther does Ella live from the library than Nick?

   (**A**) 1.36 kilometers

   (B) 1.46 kilometers

   (C) 7.86 kilometers

   (D) 42.85 kilometers

3. Rafael bought 3.26 pounds of potato salad and 2.8 pounds of macaroni salad to bring to a picnic. How much more potato salad than macaroni salad did Rafael buy?

   (A) 6.06 pounds

   (B) 2.98 pounds

   (C) 0.98 pound

   (**D**) 0.46 pound

4. Salvador had 3.25 pounds of dry cement. He used 1.7 pounds to make a paver for his lawn. How many pounds of dry cement does Salvador have left?

   (**A**) 1.55 pounds

   (B) 2.08 pounds

   (C) 3.08 pounds

   (D) 4.95 pounds

5. The community center is 4.52 miles from Molly's house and 2.81 miles from Jacob's house. Explain how Molly might regroup in order to find out how much farther she lives from the community center than Jacob.

   Possible explanation: Molly can subtract the hundredths but she needs to regroup 1 one as 10 tenths because there are not enough tenths to subtract 5 tenths. After regrouping, she can subtract 15 tenths − 8 tenths = 7 tenths, and 3 − 2 = 1. So Molly lives 1.71 miles farther from the community center than Jacob.

34   Number and Operations in Base Ten

Lesson 35
CC.5.NBT.7

1. Students are selling muffins at a school bake sale. One muffin costs $0.25, 2 muffins cost $0.37, 3 muffins cost $0.49, and 4 muffins cost $0.61. If this pattern continues, how much will 6 muffins cost?

   (A) $0.73

   (B) $0.83

   (**C**) $0.85

   (D) $0.97

2. Bob and Ling are playing a number sequence game. Bob wrote the following sequence.

   28.9, 26.8, 24.7, __?__, 20.5

   What is the unknown term in this sequence?

   (A) 21.6

   (**B**) 22.6

   (C) 22.7

   (D) 25.8

3. Students are selling handmade magnets at the school craft fair. One magnet costs $0.30, 2 magnets cost $0.43, 3 magnets cost $0.56, and 4 magnets cost $0.69. If this pattern continues, how much will 6 magnets cost?

   (A) $0.82

   (B) $0.93

   (**C**) $0.95

   (D) $1.02

4. Kevin and Yasuko are writing number sequences. Yasuko wrote the following number sequence.

   35.9, 34.7, 33.5, __?__, 31.1

   What is the unknown term in this sequence?

   (**A**) 32.3

   (B) 32.2

   (C) 32

   (D) 31.2

5. A beach resort rents snorkeling gear at $3.00 for 1 hour, $4.50 for 2 hours, $6.00 for 3 hours, and $7.50 for 4 hours. What rule could George use to find how much it will cost him to rent the gear for 6 hours? Explain how you found the rule.

   Possible answer: The rule would be to start at $3.00 and add $1.50 per hour. The costs increase by the same amount, $1.50, for each additional hour, so the rule had to include addition.

Number and Operations in Base Ten   35

Lesson 36
CC.5.NBT.7

1. At the end of October, Mr. Diamond had a balance of $367.38 in his checking account. Since then, he has written two checks for $136.94 and $14.75 and made a deposit of $185.00. What is the balance in Mr. Diamond's checking account now?

   (A) $30.69

   (B) $334.07

   (**C**) $400.69

   (D) $704.07

2. Mario has $15. If he spends $6.25 on admission to the ice skating rink, $2.95 to rent skates, and $1.65 each for 2 hot chocolates, how much money will he have left?

   (A) $2.50

   (B) $3.50

   (C) $4.15

   (**D**) $10.85

3. Miguel has $20 to spend on going to a movie. If he spends $7.25 on a movie ticket, $3.95 for snacks, and $1.75 for bus fare each way, how much money will he have left?

   (A) $14.70

   (B) $7.05

   (C) $6.30

   (**D**) $5.30

4. At the end of November, Mrs. Gold had a balance of $426.83 in her checking account. Since then, she has written two checks for $163.49 and $16.85 and made a deposit of $195.00. What is the balance in Mrs. Gold's checking account now?

   (A) $51.49

   (B) $412.17

   (**C**) $441.49

   (D) $802.17

5. Each package of stickers that Olivia wants to buy costs $1.25. Olivia has $10. Explain how you can find the number of packages of stickers Olivia can buy.

   Possible explanation: I can keep adding the cost of one package until I find how many packages add up to $10. $1.25 + $1.25 + $1.25 + $1.25 + $1.25 + $1.25 + $1.25 + $1.25 = $10. So Olivia can buy 8 packages of stickers.

36   Number and Operations in Base Ten

Answer Key

Lesson 37
CC.5.NBT.7

1. Della's cats weigh 9.8 and 8.25 pounds, and her dog weighs 25 pounds. How much more does her dog weigh than the total weight of both of her cats?

   Ⓐ 6.95 pounds
   Ⓑ 15.2 pounds
   Ⓒ 16.75 pounds
   Ⓓ 18.05 pounds

2. Rob used 4.25 ounces of peanuts, 3.4 ounces of pecans, and 2.75 ounces of walnuts to make a trail mix. How many ounces of nuts did Rob use in the trail mix?

   Ⓐ 4.1 ounces
   Ⓑ 4.865 ounces
   Ⓒ 7.34 ounces
   Ⓓ 10.4 ounces

3. Gina is training for a marathon. She ran 4.6 miles on Friday and 6.75 miles on Saturday. On Sunday, she ran 13 miles. How much farther did she run on Sunday than she did on Friday and Saturday combined?

   Ⓐ 1.65 miles
   Ⓑ 6.25 miles
   Ⓒ 11.35 miles
   Ⓓ 24.35 miles

4. Paul used 1.75 pounds of grapes, 2.6 pounds of bananas, and 3.25 pounds of apples to make fruit salad. How many pounds of fruit did Paul use in the salad?

   Ⓐ 5.26 pounds
   Ⓑ 6.6 pounds
   Ⓒ 7.6 pounds
   Ⓓ 8.6 pounds

5. William walked 2.75 miles on Friday, 3.6 miles on Saturday, and 4.25 miles on Sunday. Would you use mental math or place value to find how far William walked in all on the three days? Explain your choice.

   mental math; Possible explanation: Since 0.75 + 0.25 make 1 whole, I would use mental math. First I would add 2.75 and 4.25: 2.75 + 4.25 = 7. Then I would add 7 and 3.6: 7 + 3.6 = 10.6. William walked 10.6 miles in all on the three days.

Lesson 38
CC.5.NBT.7

1. Callie used a decimal model to help her multiply a decimal by a whole number. What equation does the model show?

   Ⓐ 3 × 0.18 = 0.54
   Ⓑ 3 × 0.18 = 5.4
   Ⓒ 18 × 0.3 = 0.54
   Ⓓ 18 × 0.3 = 5.4

2. The weight of a dime is 0.08 ounce. Amad used a model to find the weight of 7 dimes. What is the weight of 7 dimes?

   Ⓐ 0.54 ounce   Ⓒ 0.58 ounce
   Ⓑ 0.56 ounce   Ⓓ 0.78 ounce

3. Miguel used a quick picture to help him multiply a decimal by a whole number. What equation does the model show?

   Ⓐ 2 × 5.2 = 1.04
   Ⓑ 2 × 5.2 = 10.4
   Ⓒ 2 × 0.52 = 10.4
   Ⓓ 2 × 0.52 = 1.04

4. One serving of soup contains 0.45 gram of sodium. How much sodium is in 2 servings of the soup? You may use the decimal model to help you answer the question.

   Ⓐ 0.09 gram   Ⓒ 9 grams
   Ⓑ 0.9 gram   Ⓓ 90 grams

5. Ricardo walked to the library and back home. He lives 0.54 mile from the library. Draw a quick picture to find the distance Ricardo walked. Explain how you used the picture to solve the problem.

   Possible answer: I would draw 2 groups of 5 tenths and 4 hundredths. I would rename 10 hundredths as 1 tenth and cross out the renamed hundredths. I would have 1 one, and 8 hundredths, so Ricardo walked 1.08 miles.

Lesson 39
CC.5.NBT.7

1. Marci mailed 9 letters at the post office. Each letter weighed 3.5 ounces. What was the total weight of the letters that Marci mailed?

   Ⓐ 33.5 ounces
   Ⓑ 32.5 ounces
   Ⓒ 31.5 ounces
   Ⓓ 27.5 ounces

2. Laurie is in training for a race. When she trains, Laurie runs on a path that is 1.45 miles long. Last week, Laurie ran on this path 6 times. How many miles did Laurie run on the path last week?

   Ⓐ 0.87 mile
   Ⓑ 8.7 miles
   Ⓒ 87 miles
   Ⓓ 870 miles

3. Mari and Rob are making a science poster. They need to write how much a rock that weighs 7 pounds on Earth would weigh on Mars. They know they can multiply weight on Earth by 0.38 to find weight on Mars. What number should they write on their poster?

   Ⓐ 0.266 pound
   Ⓑ 2.66 pounds
   Ⓒ 26.6 pounds
   Ⓓ 266 pounds

4. Rhianna made a shelf to store her collection of rocks and shells. She used 5 pieces of wood that were each 3.25 feet long. How much wood did Rhianna use in all to make the shelf?

   Ⓐ 6.25 feet
   Ⓑ 15.05 feet
   Ⓒ 15.25 feet
   Ⓓ 16.25 feet

5. Arielle rode the Voyager roller coaster 4 times. A ride on the Voyager lasts 1.8 minutes. She rode the Cyclone roller coaster 3 times. A ride on the Cyclone lasts 2.45 minutes. Arielle says she spent more time on the Voyager than on the Cyclone. Do you agree? Support your answer.

   No; Possible answer: 1.8 × 4 = 7.2, so Arielle spent 7.2 minutes on the Voyager. 2.45 × 3 = 7.35, so Arielle spent 7.35 minutes on the Cyclone. 7.35 is greater than 7.2, so Arielle spent more time on the Cyclone than on the Voyager.

Lesson 40
CC.5.NBT.7

1. Ari is setting up a fish tank for his goldfish. The tank holds 15 gallons of water. The weight of a gallon of water rounded to the nearest tenth is 8.3 pounds. Ari used this weight to calculate the weight of the water in his fish tank. Which is the weight that Ari would find for the water in the fish tank?

   Ⓐ 12.45 pounds
   Ⓑ 16.5 pounds
   Ⓒ 124.5 pounds
   Ⓓ 165 pounds

2. Paul works at the local grocery store. He worked 15 hours this week. Last week, he worked 2.5 times as many hours as he worked this week. How many hours did Paul work last week?

   Ⓐ 30.5 hours
   Ⓑ 32.5 hours
   Ⓒ 35 hours
   Ⓓ 37.5 hours

3. The Barbers are keeping track of their family energy costs. It costs the Barbers $0.16 per week to run their dishwasher. How much will it cost them to run their dishwasher for 52 weeks?

   Ⓐ $8.64
   Ⓑ $8.32
   Ⓒ $3.64
   Ⓓ $1.92

4. Mrs. Green needs to store 21 math books on a shelf during school vacation. Each math book is 2.4 centimeters thick. If Mrs. Green stacks the math books on top of each other, how tall does the shelf have to be?

   Ⓐ 12.6 centimeters
   Ⓑ 40.4 centimeters
   Ⓒ 50.4 centimeters
   Ⓓ 54 centimeters

5. Sophia exchanged 1,000 U.S. dollars for the South African currency, which is called rand. The exchange rate was 7.15 rand to $1. How many South African rand did Sophia get? Explain how you know.

   7,150 rand; Possible explanation: for every $1 that Sophia exchanges she will get 7.15 rand. So, I multiplied $1,000 by 7.15 and got 7,150 rand.

Answer Key

Lesson 41
CC.5.NBT.7

1. At a dry cleaning store, it costs $1.79 to clean a man's dress shirt and $8.25 to clean a suit. Thomas brought in 4 shirts and 1 suit to be cleaned. How much will he be charged for the dry cleaning?

Ⓐ $15.41
Ⓑ $10.04
Ⓒ $8.95
Ⓓ $7.16

3. Tim wants to rent a bike at the state park. It costs $3.95 per hour for the first 4 hours. After 4 hours, the cost is $2.50 per hour. How much would it cost Tim to rent a bike for 5 hours?

Ⓐ $19.75
Ⓑ $18.30
Ⓒ $15.80
Ⓓ $12.50

2. Mandy, Jeremy, and Lily went to an amusement park during their summer vacation. Mandy spent $16.25 at the amusement park. Jeremy spent $3.40 more than Mandy spent. Lily spent 2 times as much money as Jeremy spent. How much money did Lily spend at the amusement park?

Ⓐ $6.80   Ⓒ $32.50
Ⓑ $19.65   Ⓓ $39.30

4. Peter spent $32.50 at the ballpark. Marty spent 5 times as much money as Peter spent. Callie spent $27.25 more than Marty. How much did Callie spend at the ballpark?

Ⓐ $59.75
Ⓑ $136.25
Ⓒ $162.50
Ⓓ $189.75

5. Chris collected $25.65 for a fundraiser. Remy collected $15.87 more than Chris did. Sandy collected 3 times as much as Remy. How much did Sandy collect for the fundraiser? Draw a diagram to solve. Then explain how you found your answer.

$25.65	$25.65	$15.87		$41.52	$41.52	$41.52
Chris	Remy				Sandy	

$124.56; Possible explanation: I drew a diagram with one box for Chris showing $25.65 and two boxes for Remy showing $25.65 and $15.87. I added them to get $41.52. Then I drew 3 boxes for Sandy and multiplied 3 × $41.52 to get $124.56.

Lesson 42
CC.5.NBT.7

1. Keisha used this decimal model to help her multiply. What equation does the model show?

Ⓐ 4 × 7 = 28   Ⓒ 0.4 × 0.7 = 0.28
Ⓑ 4 × 0.7 = 2.8   Ⓓ 0.4 × 7 = 2.8

3. Mickey used a decimal model to help him multiply 0.3 × 0.8. What is the product of 0.3 and 0.8?

Ⓐ 0.024   Ⓒ 2.4
Ⓑ 0.24   Ⓓ 24

2. Lorenzo had a piece of wire that was 0.6 meter long. He used 0.5 of the wire. How much wire did Lorenzo use?

Ⓐ 0.03 meter   Ⓒ 0.3 meter
Ⓑ 0.1 meter   Ⓓ 1.1 meters

4. One serving of a dried fruit mix contains 0.9 gram of potassium. How much potassium is in 0.5 serving of the dried fruit mix? You may use the decimal model to help you answer the question.

Ⓐ 0.45 gram   Ⓒ 4.5 grams
Ⓑ 1.4 grams   Ⓓ 45 grams

5. Arina bought 0.9 yard of material. She used 0.8 of the material to make place mats. Use the decimal model to show how much material she used. Then explain how you found the answer.

Possible answer: I would shade 9 columns of a decimal model to represent 0.9. Then I would shade 8 rows to represent 0.8. The shadings overlap in 72 squares, or 0.72.

Lesson 43
CC.5.NBT.7

1. A scientist at a giant panda preserve in China measured the length of a newborn cub as 15.5 centimeters. The cub's mother was 9.5 times as tall as the length of the cub. How tall is the mother?

Ⓐ 14.725 centimeters
Ⓑ 25 centimeters
Ⓒ 147.25 centimeters
Ⓓ 1,472.5 centimeters

3. Mel's father asked Mel to mow his lawn while he was on vacation. Mel bought 1.6 gallons of gas for the lawn mower. The gas cost $2.85 per gallon. How much money did Mel pay for the gas?

Ⓐ $45.60
Ⓑ $4.56
Ⓒ $4.45
Ⓓ $4.13

2. Emily stopped at a produce stand to buy some tomatoes. Tomatoes cost $1.25 per pound at the stand. Emily bought 5 tomatoes that weighed a total of 1.8 pounds. How much did Emily pay for the tomatoes?

Ⓐ $2.25
Ⓑ $3.05
Ⓒ $6.25
Ⓓ $22.50

4. Mr. Harris has 54.8 acres of land. Mr. Fitz has 0.35 as many acres as Mr. Harris has. How many acres of land does Mr. Fitz have?

Ⓐ 4.384 acres
Ⓑ 19.108 acres
Ⓒ 19.18 acres
Ⓓ 43.84 acres

5. Mr. Evans is paid $9.20 per hour for the first 40 hours he works in a week. He is paid 1.5 times that rate for each hour he works after that. Last week Mr. Evans worked 42.25 hours. He says he earned more than $400 last week. Do you agree? Support your answer.

I disagree; Possible explanation: $9.20 × 40 = $368, which is the earnings for 40 hours. $9.20 × 1.5 = $13.80, which is the overtime rate. $13.80 × 2.25 = $31.05. I added $31.05 + $368 = $399.05. $399.05 < $400.

Lesson 44
CC.5.NBT.7

1. Denise, Keith, and Tim live in the same neighborhood. Denise lives 0.3 mile from Keith. The distance that Tim and Keith live from each other is 0.2 times longer than the distance between Denise and Keith. How far from each other do Tim and Keith live?

Ⓐ 0.6 mile
Ⓑ 0.5 mile
Ⓒ 0.1 mile
Ⓓ 0.06 mile

3. The information booklet for a video console says that the console uses about 0.2 kilowatt of electricity per hour. If electricity costs $0.15 per kilowatt hour, how much does it cost to run the console for an hour?

Ⓐ $0.03
Ⓑ $0.30
Ⓒ $3.00
Ⓓ $30.00

2. Tina is making a special dessert for her brother's birthday. Tina's recipe calls for 0.5 kilogram of flour. The recipe also calls for an amount of sugar that is 0.8 times as much as the amount of flour. How much sugar will Tina need to make the dessert?

Ⓐ 4 kilograms
Ⓑ 0.4 kilogram
Ⓒ 0.04 kilogram
Ⓓ 0.004 kilogram

4. Bruce is getting materials for a chemistry experiment. His teacher gives him a container that holds 0.25 liter of a blue liquid. Bruce needs to use 0.4 of this liquid for the experiment. How much blue liquid will Bruce use?

Ⓐ 0.001 liter
Ⓑ 0.01 liter
Ⓒ 0.1 liter
Ⓓ 1 liter

5. Ashton bought a new laptop computer that uses about 0.4 kilowatt of electricity per hour. Electricity costs $0.10 per kilowatt hour. Explain how you can find how much it costs to use the laptop for one hour.

Possible explanation: multiply as with whole numbers. 10 × 4 = 40. There are 2 decimal places in $0.10 and 1 decimal place in 0.4, so there will be 2 + 1, or 3 decimal places in the product. I would write a zero to the left of the 40 to place the decimal point. $0.10 × 0.4 = $0.040, or $0.04.

Answer Key

Lesson 45
CC.5.NBT.7

1. Emilio used a model to help him divide 2.46 by 2. What is the quotient?

(A) 1.23
(B) 1.32
(C) 3.21
(D) 12.3

2. Heath bought 1.2 pounds of potato salad. He divided it into 4 containers, each with the same amount. How much potato salad was in each container?

(A) 0.03 pound
(B) 0.3 pound
(C) 0.8 pound
(D) 4.8 pounds

3. Theo made a model to represent a division statement. What division statement does the model show?

(A) 3.12 ÷ 3 = 1.12
(B) 3.63 ÷ 3 = 1.21
(C) 2.24 ÷ 2 = 1.12
(D) 3.36 ÷ 3 = 1.12

4. Maya practiced the piano for 3.75 hours last week. If she practiced the same amount of time each of 5 days, how long did she practice each day?

(A) 0.25 hour
(B) 0.5 hour
(C) 0.75 hour
(D) 1.25 hours

5. Nina bought 3.24 pounds of ground beef and made 3 packages from it. Each package had the same amount of ground beef. How can you use base-ten blocks to model how much ground beef Nina put in each package?

Possible answer: I can use 3 ones blocks, 2 tenths blocks, and 4 hundredths blocks to model 3.24. There are not enough tenths blocks to share among 3 packages, so I can replace each of them with 10 hundredths blocks to make 24 hundredths blocks. There will be 1 ones block and 8 hundredths blocks in each group. 3.24 ÷ 3 = 1.08.

Number and Operations in Base Ten   45

Lesson 46
CC.5.NBT.7

1. Ashleigh rode her bicycle 26.5 miles in 4 hours. Which gives the **best** estimate of how far Ashleigh rode in 1 hour?

(A) 0.5 mile
(B) 0.6 mile
(C) 5 miles
(D) 7 miles

2. Ellen drove 357.9 miles. Her car gets about 21 miles per gallon. Which is the **best** estimate of how many gallons of gas Ellen used?

(A) 17 gallons
(B) 16 gallons
(C) 1.7 gallons
(D) 0.17 gallon

3. Landon bought a box of plants for $8.79. There were 16 plants in the box. If Landon had bought only 1 plant, about how much would it have cost?

(A) about $0.40
(B) about $0.50
(C) about $0.60
(D) about $0.70

4. Josh bought a 34.6-pound bag of dry dog food to feed his dogs. The bag lasted 8 days. About how much dog food did his dogs eat each day?

(A) about 0.4 pound
(B) about 0.5 pound
(C) about 4 pounds
(D) about 5 pounds

5. Karl drove 624.3 miles. He used a total of 31 gallons of gas in his car. How can Karl estimate how many miles per gallon his car gets?

Possible explanation: Karl can round 31 to 30. Find a number close to and greater than 624.3 that divides easily by 30: 630 ÷ 30 = 21. Find a number close to and less than 624.3: 600 ÷ 30 = 20. Karl's car gets more than 20 but less than 21 miles per gallon.

46   Number and Operations in Base Ten

Lesson 47
CC.5.NBT.7

1. Grant is making small bags of dried fruit from a large bag of dried fruit that weighs 5.46 pounds. If he puts the same amount of dried fruit in each of 6 bags, how much will each bag weigh?

(A) 0.0091 pound
(B) 0.091 pound
(C) 0.91 pound
(D) 9.1 pounds

2. Mia has a piece of ribbon that is 30.5 yards long. The length is just enough ribbon to make 5 bows that are the same size. How long is the ribbon that she uses for each bow?

(A) 6.01 yards
(B) 6.1 yards
(C) 6.2 yards
(D) 6.5 yards

3. A plumber has a piece of copper tubing that is 112.8 inches long. He needs to cut the tubing into 12 equal pieces to repair some leaky pipes. How long will each piece of tubing be?

(A) 0.094 inch
(B) 0.94 inch
(C) 9.4 inches
(D) 94 inches

4. Matthew bought 13 used video games that were on sale in a store. He paid $84.37 for the games. If each video game cost the same price, how much did 1 video game cost?

(A) $6.09
(B) $6.19
(C) $6.39
(D) $6.49

5. Chase can buy a pack of baseball cards that contains 24 cards for $3.84, or he can buy a pack that contains 60 cards for $8.40. Chase wants to buy the pack of baseball cards that is the better buy. Which pack should he buy? Support your answer.

60 cards for $8.40; Possible explanation:
$3.84 ÷ 24 = $0.16 per card. $8.40 ÷ 60 = $0.14 per card. The better buy would be 60 cards for $8.40 since the cost per card is less.

Number and Operations in Base Ten   47

Lesson 48
CC.5.NBT.7

1. Peter used a model to help him divide 0.28 by 0.07. What is the quotient?

(A) 0.04
(B) 0.4
(C) 4
(D) 28

2. Heather used 1.5 pounds of roast beef. She used 0.5 pound in each sandwich. How many sandwiches did she make?

(A) 0.3
(B) 3
(C) 4.5
(D) 30

3. Fiona made the model below to represent a division statement. What division statement does the model show?

(A) 1.2 ÷ 0.3 = 4
(B) 1.2 ÷ 0.4 = 3
(C) 1.6 ÷ 0.4 = 4
(D) 0.9 ÷ 0.3 = 3

4. Tyrone used 3.75 cups of hot water to make hot chocolate. He poured 0.75 cup of hot water into each mug of chocolate. How many mugs of hot chocolate did he make?

(A) 3
(B) 4
(C) 5
(D) 6

5. Eddie paid $0.80 for some pencils. Each pencil cost $0.16. Explain how to use a model to find how many pencils Eddie bought.

Possible explanation: I would shade 80 squares of a hundredths model to represent the dividend, 0.80. Then I would divide the 80 hundredths into equal-sized groups of 16 to represent the divisor, 0.16. My model would show 5 groups of 16, so, Eddie bought 5 pencils.

48   Number and Operations in Base Ten

Answer Key

1. Leilani bought tomatoes that cost $0.84 per pound. She paid $3.36 for the tomatoes. How many pounds of tomatoes did she buy?

   (A) 0.004 pound
   (B) 0.04 pound
   (C) 0.4 pound
   (D) 4 pounds

3. Latisha hiked along a trail that was 9.66 miles long last Saturday. It took her 4.2 hours to complete the trail. What was Latisha's average speed per hour?

   (A) 0.23 mile per hour
   (B) 2.3 miles per hour
   (C) 20.3 miles per hour
   (D) 23 miles per hour

2. Carly has a piece of yarn that is 7.2 yards long. She needs to cut the yarn into pieces of fringe that each measure 0.3 yard long. How many pieces of fringe can she cut from the piece of yarn?

   (A) 2,400
   (B) 240
   (C) 24
   (D) 2.4

4. Quan records that his hamster can turn the wheel in its cage to make 1 revolution in 0.5 minute. How many revolutions can the hamster make in 20.5 minutes?

   (A) 4.1
   (B) 41
   (C) 410
   (D) 4,100

5. Shareen walked a total of 9.52 miles in a walk-a-thon. She completed the walk in 3.4 hours. She wanted to find her average walking speed. Explain why Shareen might begin by multiplying 3.4 and 9.52 by the same power of ten to solve the problem.

   Possible explanation: to find her average speed, she has to

   divide 9.52 by 3.4. If she multiplies the divisor by a power

   of 10 to make it a whole number and multiplies the dividend

   by the same power of 10, she has a simpler division

   problem and the quotient will be the same as if she

   divided the decimals.

---

1. Tony collected 16.2 pounds of pecans from the trees at his farm. He will give the same weight of pecans to each of 12 friends. How many pounds of pecans will each friend get?

   (A) 0.135 pound
   (B) 1.35 pounds
   (C) 13.5 pounds
   (D) 135 pounds

3. Denise's mother bought some zucchini for $0.78 per pound. If she paid $2.73 for the zucchini, how many pounds of zucchini did she buy?

   (A) 0.35 pound
   (B) 3.5 pounds
   (C) 35 pounds
   (D) 350 pounds

2. Trevor drove 202 miles to visit his grandparents. It took him 4 hours to get there. What was the average speed that Trevor drove?

   (A) 5.05 miles per hour
   (B) 5.5 miles per hour
   (C) 50.5 miles per hour
   (D) 55 miles per hour

4. The students at Winwood Elementary School collected 574 cans of food in 20 days for a food drive. What was the average number of cans of food collected each day?

   (A) 2.87
   (B) 27
   (C) 28
   (D) 28.7

5. Cynthia bought some grapes on sale for $0.94 per pound. She paid $2.35 for the grapes. Cynthia said that she bought between 2 and 3 pounds of grapes. Do you agree with Cynthia? Support your answer.

   I agree; Possible explanation: I divided $2.35 by $0.94.

   I moved the decimal point two places to the right in

   both the divisor and the dividend: 235 ÷ 94. I placed a

   decimal point in the quotient above the decimal point

   in the dividend, which was after the 5 in 235. 94 does

   not divide evenly into 235, so I wrote a zero to the right

   of the decimal point in the dividend and continued

   dividing. 235 ÷ 94 = 2.5; 2.5 is between 2 and 3.

---

1. Reshawn is buying 3 books in a set for $24.81. He will save $6.69 by buying the set instead of buying individual books. If each book costs the same amount, how much does each of the 3 books cost when purchased individually?

   (A) $2.23
   (B) $6.04
   (C) $8.27
   (D) $10.50

3. Corey and Nicole spent $17.00, including sales tax, on 2 sandwiches and 3 slices of pizza. The sandwiches cost $5.25 each and the total sales tax was $0.92. How much did each slice of pizza cost?

   (A) $1.86
   (B) $2.47
   (C) $2.79
   (D) $5.58

2. Mackenzie spent a total of $17.50 on Saturday afternoon. She bought a movie ticket for $7.25 and snacks for $4.95. She spent the rest of the money on bus fare to get to the movie and back home. How much was the bus fare each way if each trip cost the same amount?

   (A) $2.60   (C) $5.20
   (B) $2.65   (D) $5.30

4. Jocelyn bought 2 sweaters for the same price. She paid $23.56, including sales tax of $1.36 and a $5.00 coupon. What was the price of one sweater before the tax and coupon?

   (A) $8.60
   (B) $19.96
   (C) $13.60
   (D) $14.96

5. Samantha bought flowers at a craft store for $14.02. She also bought 4 packages of glass beads and 2 vases. The vases cost $3.59 each and the total sales tax was $1.34. The total amount she paid was $28.50, including sales tax. Explain a strategy you would use to find the cost of one package of glass beads.

   Possible explanation: I would make the following flowchart:

   cost of 4 packages of glass beads + cost of flowers + cost of

   2 vases + sales tax = Total Spent. Then I would work backward

   to find the cost of the 4 packages of glass beads: Total spent

   − sales tax − cost of 2 vases − cost of flowers = cost of

   4 packages of glass beads. Then I would divide the cost of the

   4 packages of glass beads by 4 to find the cost of 1 package.

---

1. Arturo wants to find the amount of time he spent on his math and science homework combined. He worked $\frac{2}{5}$ hour on math and $\frac{1}{3}$ hour on science. Which is the **best** strategy to find the least common denominator so he can add the time he spent on his homework?

   (A) Multiply denominators since they share no common factors other than 1.
   (B) Find all the multiples of each denominator.
   (C) One denominator is the multiple of the other, so the multiple is the least common denominator.
   (D) Add the denominators to find the least common multiple.

2. Francine wants to find the total of $\frac{2}{3}$ cup of blueberries and $\frac{5}{8}$ cup of raspberries. What is the least common denominator of the fractions?

   (A) 10   (C) 18
   (B) 11   (D) 24

3. Alana bought $\frac{3}{8}$ pound of Swiss cheese and $\frac{1}{4}$ pound of American cheese. Which pair of fractions **cannot** be used to find how many pounds of cheese she bought in all?

   (A) $\frac{6}{16}$ and $\frac{4}{16}$
   (B) $\frac{9}{24}$ and $\frac{6}{24}$
   (C) $\frac{24}{64}$ and $\frac{8}{64}$
   (D) $\frac{15}{40}$ and $\frac{10}{40}$

4. Charles bought $\frac{7}{8}$ foot of electrical wire and $\frac{5}{6}$ foot of copper wire for his science project. What is the least common denominator of the fractions?

   (A) 14
   (B) 18
   (C) 24
   (D) 48

5. On Saturday, Percy biked for $6\frac{3}{12}$ hours. On Sunday, he biked for $5\frac{2}{3}$ hours. Explain how to find the least common denominator of these two fractions.

   Possible answer: find the least common denominator for

   3 and 12 by listing the multiples of 3: 3, 6, 9, 12, 15. Since

   12 is a multiple of 3, it is the least common denominator

   of 3 and 12

Answer Key   **113**

Name _____

1. Brady used $\frac{2}{3}$ gallon of yellow paint and $\frac{1}{4}$ gallon of white paint to paint his dresser. How many gallons of paint did Brady use?

Ⓐ $\frac{3}{7}$ gallon

Ⓑ $\frac{3}{4}$ gallon

Ⓒ $\frac{5}{6}$ gallon

Ⓓ $\frac{11}{12}$ gallon

2. Mr. Barber uses $\frac{7}{9}$ yard of wire to put up a ceiling fan. He uses $\frac{1}{3}$ yard of wire to fix a switch. How much more wire does he use to put up the fan than to fix the switch?

Ⓐ $1\frac{1}{9}$ yards

Ⓑ $\frac{9}{9}$ yard

Ⓒ $\frac{4}{9}$ yard

Ⓓ $\frac{1}{3}$ yard

3. Tom jogged $\frac{3}{5}$ mile on Monday and $\frac{2}{6}$ mile on Tuesday. How much farther did Tom jog on Monday than on Tuesday?

Ⓐ $\frac{1}{30}$ mile

Ⓑ $\frac{3}{15}$ mile

Ⓒ $\frac{8}{30}$ mile

Ⓓ $\frac{14}{15}$ mile

4. Mindy bought $\frac{1}{6}$ pound of almonds and $\frac{3}{4}$ pound of walnuts. How many pounds of nuts did she buy in all?

Ⓐ $\frac{1}{3}$

Ⓑ $\frac{7}{12}$

Ⓒ $\frac{4}{5}$

Ⓓ $\frac{11}{12}$

5. George worked on his science project for $\frac{5}{12}$ hour on Monday and $\frac{3}{4}$ hour on Tuesday. How much longer did George work on his science project on Tuesday than on Monday? Explain how you found your answer.

$\frac{1}{3}$ hour longer; Possible explanation: I found a common denominator for 12 and 4 and wrote equivalent fractions. $\frac{5}{12} = \frac{5}{12}$ and $\frac{3}{4} = \frac{9}{12}$. Then I subtracted: $\frac{9}{12} - \frac{5}{12} = \frac{4}{12}$. I simplified my answer: $\frac{4}{12} = \frac{1}{3}$.

Number and Operations–Fractions

53

Name _____

1. David practices piano for $1\frac{1}{3}$ hours on Monday and $3\frac{1}{2}$ hours on Tuesday. How much longer does he practice piano on Tuesday than on Monday?

Ⓐ $1\frac{1}{5}$ hours

Ⓑ $2\frac{1}{6}$ hours

Ⓒ $2\frac{2}{5}$ hours

Ⓓ $2\frac{5}{6}$ hours

2. Roberto's cat weighed $6\frac{3}{4}$ pounds last year. The cat weighs $1\frac{1}{2}$ pounds more now. How much does the cat weigh now?

Ⓐ $5\frac{1}{4}$ pounds

Ⓑ $7\frac{1}{4}$ pounds

Ⓒ $7\frac{3}{4}$ pounds

Ⓓ $8\frac{1}{4}$ pounds

3. Ken bought $3\frac{3}{4}$ pounds of apples at the farmers' market. Abby bought $2\frac{1}{8}$ pounds of apples. How many pounds of apples did Ken and Abby buy in all?

Ⓐ $5\frac{1}{8}$ pounds   Ⓒ $5\frac{7}{8}$ pounds

Ⓑ $5\frac{1}{3}$ pounds   Ⓓ $6\frac{1}{4}$ pounds

4. Three students made videos for their art project. The table shows the length of each video.

Art in Nature

Video	Length (in hours)
1	$4\frac{3}{4}$
2	$2\frac{7}{12}$
3	$2\frac{1}{6}$

How much longer is video 1 than video 3?

Ⓐ $1\frac{5}{12}$ hours   Ⓒ $2\frac{5}{12}$ hours

Ⓑ $1\frac{7}{12}$ hours   Ⓓ $2\frac{7}{12}$ hours

5. It takes Evan $6\frac{3}{4}$ hours to mow 3 lawns. It takes him $2\frac{1}{3}$ hours to mow Mr. Garcia's lawn and $1\frac{3}{4}$ hours to mow Miss Pasteur's lawn. How many hours does it take Evan to mow the third lawn? Explain how you found your answer.

$2\frac{2}{3}$ hours. I first added the times for Mr. Garcia's and Miss Pasteur's lawns, $2\frac{1}{3}$ hour and $1\frac{3}{4}$ hour, by finding the least common denominator, 12. I renamed $2\frac{1}{3}$ as $2\frac{4}{12}$, and renamed $1\frac{3}{4}$ as $1\frac{9}{12}$, then added $2\frac{4}{12} + 1\frac{9}{12} = 3\frac{13}{12}$, or $4\frac{1}{12}$. I then renamed the total, $6\frac{3}{4}$, as $6\frac{9}{12}$, and subtracted; $6\frac{9}{12} - 4\frac{1}{12} = 2\frac{8}{12} = 2\frac{2}{3}$.

54

Number and Operations–Fractions

Name _____

1. Kyle is hanging wallpaper in his bedroom. A roll of wallpaper is $18\frac{3}{8}$ feet long. Kyle cut off a piece of wallpaper $2\frac{5}{6}$ feet long. How much wallpaper is left on the roll?

Ⓐ $15\frac{13}{24}$ feet

Ⓑ $15\frac{7}{12}$ feet

Ⓒ $16\frac{13}{24}$ feet

Ⓓ $17\frac{3}{8}$ feet

2. Giselle made $24\frac{1}{8}$ ounces of lemonade. She sampled $1\frac{1}{2}$ ounces to make sure it is not too sour. How much lemonade is left?

Ⓐ $23\frac{5}{8}$ ounces

Ⓑ $23\frac{5}{6}$ ounces

Ⓒ $22\frac{5}{8}$ ounces

Ⓓ $22\frac{5}{16}$ ounces

3. Maria needs a piece of string $4\frac{2}{3}$ feet long for a science project. She cuts it from a piece that is $7\frac{1}{12}$ feet long. How much string does she have left?

Ⓐ $11\frac{3}{4}$ feet

Ⓑ $3\frac{5}{12}$ feet

Ⓒ $2\frac{7}{12}$ feet

Ⓓ $2\frac{5}{12}$ feet

4. Taylor saw an American alligator at a zoo that measured $12\frac{11}{12}$ feet long. The record length of an American alligator is $19\frac{1}{6}$ feet long. How much longer is the record alligator than the alligator Taylor saw?

Ⓐ $5\frac{5}{8}$ feet

Ⓑ $5\frac{7}{8}$ feet

Ⓒ $6\frac{1}{4}$ feet

Ⓓ $6\frac{1}{8}$ feet

5. Mr. Carlson has $1\frac{3}{8}$ acres of land. His house and yard cover $\frac{7}{8}$ acre and he uses the rest of his land to grow corn. Mr. Carlson states that he uses most of his land to grow corn. Describe Mr. Carlson's statement as true or false, and explain why.

It is false. The total amount of land minus the amount used for his house and yard is $1\frac{3}{8} - \frac{7}{8} = \frac{11}{8} - \frac{7}{8} = \frac{4}{8}$. So the amount used for the house and yard, $\frac{7}{8}$, is more than the amount of land used to grow corn, $\frac{4}{8}$.

Number and Operations–Fractions

55

Name _____

1. Carrie is given a plant. After one week, it grows to $\frac{7}{8}$ foot tall, and after two weeks it grows to $1\frac{1}{2}$ feet tall. If it keeps growing at the same pace, how tall will it be after 3 weeks?

Ⓐ $2\frac{1}{4}$ feet

Ⓑ $2\frac{1}{8}$ feet

Ⓒ $1\frac{7}{8}$ feet

Ⓓ $1\frac{5}{8}$ feet

2. Chan ran a race course in $1\frac{3}{5}$ hours. The following month, he ran the same course in $1\frac{3}{10}$ hours. If his time improves by the same amount each month, how long will it take to run the course after another month?

Ⓐ $\frac{4}{5}$ hour

Ⓑ $\frac{9}{10}$ hour

Ⓒ 1 hour

Ⓓ $1\frac{1}{5}$ hours

3. When Bruce started bowling, he won $\frac{1}{4}$ of the games he played. Within six months, he was winning $\frac{7}{16}$ of his games. If he improves at the same rate, what fraction of his games should he expect to win after another six months?

Ⓐ $\frac{1}{2}$

Ⓑ $\frac{9}{16}$

Ⓒ $\frac{5}{8}$

Ⓓ $\frac{11}{16}$

4. A farm produced $1\frac{1}{6}$ tons of corn in its first year, $1\frac{3}{8}$ tons in its second year, and $1\frac{10}{16}$ tons in its third year. If the pattern continues each year, how much corn did the farm produce in the fourth year?

Ⓐ $1\frac{12}{16}$ tons

Ⓑ $1\frac{7}{8}$ tons

Ⓒ $1\frac{3}{4}$ tons

Ⓓ $1\frac{5}{16}$ tons

5. When Jill started jogging, she ran $\frac{3}{4}$ mile on the first day, $1\frac{1}{8}$ miles on the second day, and $1\frac{1}{2}$ miles on the third day. If she increases the distance she jogs each day by the same amount, how far will she jog on the fifth day? Explain how you found your answer.

$2\frac{1}{4}$ miles; Possible explanation: the difference between how far Jill jogged on the first day and second day is $\frac{3}{8}$ mile and the difference between how far she jogged on the second day and third day is $\frac{3}{8}$ mile. I added $\frac{3}{8}$ to $1\frac{1}{2}$ and got $1\frac{7}{8}$ for the fourth day. Then I added $\frac{3}{8}$ to $1\frac{7}{8}$ and got $2\frac{1}{4}$ miles for the fifth day.

56

Number and Operations–Fractions

Answer Key

1. Ava hiked a trail that has three sections that are $4\frac{7}{8}$ miles, $3\frac{3}{8}$ miles, and $5\frac{1}{8}$ miles long. Ava wrote this expression to show the total distance that she hiked.

$$\left(4\frac{7}{8} + 3\frac{3}{8}\right) + 5\frac{1}{8}$$

Which shows another way to write the expression using only the Commutative Property of Addition?

- Ⓐ $4\frac{7}{8} + \left(3\frac{3}{8} + 5\frac{1}{8}\right)$
- Ⓑ $\left(5\frac{1}{8} + 4\frac{7}{8}\right) + 3\frac{3}{8}$
- Ⓒ $\left(3\frac{3}{4} + 4\frac{7}{8}\right) + 5\frac{1}{8}$
- Ⓓ $(4 + 3 + 5) + \left(\frac{7}{8} + \frac{4}{8} + \frac{1}{8}\right)$

2. Shelley wove three rugs with geometric designs. She wrote this expression to show the total length in feet of all three rugs.

$$\left(8\frac{7}{16} + 11\frac{7}{8}\right) + 15\frac{1}{4}$$

Which shows another way to write the expression using the Associative Property of Addition?

- Ⓐ $8\frac{7}{16} + \left(15\frac{7}{4} + 11\frac{1}{4}\right)$
- Ⓑ $8\frac{7}{16} + \left(11\frac{7}{8} + 15\frac{1}{4}\right)$
- Ⓒ $\left(8\frac{7}{16} + 11\frac{7}{8}\right) + \left(8\frac{7}{16} + 15\frac{1}{4}\right)$
- Ⓓ $(8 + 11 + 15) + \left(\frac{7}{16} + \frac{7}{8} + \frac{1}{4}\right)$

3. Larry wrote this expression to show the total number of hours he spent driving during the last three weeks.

$$\left(5\frac{2}{5} + 7\frac{4}{10}\right) + 9\frac{1}{10}$$

Which shows another way to write the expression using the Associative Property of Addition?

- Ⓐ $5\frac{2}{5} + \left(7\frac{4}{10} + 9\frac{1}{10}\right)$
- Ⓑ $5\frac{2}{5} + \left(9\frac{1}{10} + 7\frac{4}{10}\right)$
- Ⓒ $\left(7\frac{4}{10} + 9\frac{1}{10}\right) + 5\frac{2}{5}$
- Ⓓ $(5 + 9 + 4) + \left(\frac{2}{5} + \frac{4}{10} + \frac{1}{10}\right)$

4. Marco wrote the following expression to find the total amount of gasoline he bought last month.

$$8\frac{1}{5} + 6\frac{1}{8} + 7\frac{3}{5}$$

Which expression will help make the addition easier for Marco?

- Ⓐ $\left(8\frac{1}{5} + 6\frac{1}{8}\right) + 7\frac{3}{5}$
- Ⓑ $\left(7\frac{3}{8} + 6\frac{1}{8}\right) + 8\frac{1}{5}$
- Ⓒ $\left(8\frac{1}{5} + 7\frac{3}{5}\right) + 6\frac{1}{8}$
- Ⓓ $\left(8\frac{1}{5} + 7\frac{3}{5}\right) + 6\frac{1}{8}$

5. Stephen has three fish tanks that hold $5\frac{2}{3}$ gallons, $3\frac{5}{8}$ gallons, and $4\frac{1}{3}$ gallons. He wants to put the water from the three tanks into one new tank. Explain the easiest way for him to find the minimum size the new tank should be.

The easiest way is to add all the numbers. Add the

numbers with the same denominator first, $5\frac{2}{3}$ and $4\frac{1}{3} = 9\frac{3}{3}$,

or 10. Then, add the last number, $10 + 3\frac{5}{8} = 13\frac{5}{8}$ gallons.

Use the information for 1-2.

Addison used $\frac{5}{6}$ yard of ribbon to decorate a photo frame. She used $\frac{1}{3}$ yard of ribbon to decorate her scrapbook.

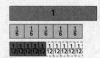

1. Which fraction strips should Addison trade for the $\frac{1}{3}$ strip in order to find how many yards of ribbon she used in all?

- Ⓐ $\frac{1}{2}$
- Ⓒ $\frac{1}{4}$
- Ⓑ $\frac{1}{3}$
- Ⓓ $\frac{1}{6}$

2. How many yards of ribbon did Addison use in all?

- Ⓐ $1\frac{1}{6}$ yards
- Ⓒ $\frac{5}{9}$ yard
- Ⓑ 1 yard
- Ⓓ $\frac{1}{2}$ yard

Use the information for 3-4.

Gabrielle paints a flower pot to sell at the craft fair. She paints $\frac{2}{5}$ of the pot teal, $\frac{3}{10}$ of the pot yellow, and the rest of the pot white.

3. Which fraction strips should Gabrielle trade for the $\frac{2}{5}$ strip in order to find how much of the pot is painted teal or yellow?

- Ⓐ $\frac{1}{2}$
- Ⓒ $\frac{1}{10}$
- Ⓑ $\frac{1}{5}$
- Ⓓ $\frac{1}{15}$

4. How much of the pot is painted teal or yellow?

- Ⓐ $\frac{1}{10}$
- Ⓒ $\frac{1}{2}$
- Ⓑ $\frac{5}{15}$
- Ⓓ $\frac{7}{10}$

5. Juan needs $\frac{1}{4}$ cup of flour to make muffins and $\frac{3}{8}$ cup to make brownies. Draw fraction strips to help you find the total amount of flour Juan needs. Explain your work.

Juan needs $\frac{5}{8}$ cup of flour to make the muffins and

brownies. I drew fraction strips for $\frac{1}{4}$ and $\frac{3}{8}$. Then I

drew $\frac{2}{8}$ to replace the $\frac{1}{4}$, and added: $\frac{2}{8} + \frac{3}{8} = \frac{5}{8}$.

Use the information for 1-2.

Armand lives $\frac{7}{8}$ mile from school. On his way home from school, he rode his skateboard $\frac{5}{16}$ mile and walked the rest of the way.

1. How many $\frac{1}{16}$ fraction strips are equal to $\frac{7}{8}$?

- Ⓐ 5
- Ⓒ 8
- Ⓑ 7
- Ⓓ 14

2. How far did Armand walk?

- Ⓐ $\frac{1}{8}$ mile
- Ⓒ $\frac{9}{16}$ mile
- Ⓑ $\frac{1}{2}$ mile
- Ⓓ $1\frac{1}{8}$ miles

Use the information for 3-4.

Kim has a piece of cardboard that is $\frac{5}{6}$ inch long. She cut off a $\frac{5}{12}$-inch piece.

3. How many $\frac{1}{12}$ fraction strips are equal to $\frac{5}{6}$?

- Ⓐ 5
- Ⓒ 10
- Ⓑ 6
- Ⓓ 12

4. How long is the remaining piece of cardboard?

- Ⓐ $\frac{10}{12}$ inch
- Ⓒ $\frac{1}{3}$ inch
- Ⓑ $\frac{5}{12}$ inch
- Ⓓ $\frac{1}{6}$ inch

5. Ami spent $\frac{5}{6}$ hour doing math and science homework, with $\frac{1}{4}$ hour spent on math. Draw fraction strips to help you find how much time Ami spent on science homework. Explain your work.

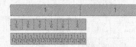

Ami spent $\frac{7}{12}$ hour on science homework. I drew fraction

strips for $\frac{5}{6}$ and $\frac{3}{12}$. Then I drew $\frac{10}{12}$ to replace the $\frac{5}{6}$, and $\frac{3}{12}$

to replace the $\frac{1}{4}$. I subtracted: $\frac{10}{12} - \frac{3}{12} = \frac{7}{12}$.

---

1. Ron walked $\frac{8}{10}$ mile from his grandmother's house to the store. Then he walked $\frac{9}{10}$ mile to his house. About how far did he walk altogether?

- Ⓐ about $\frac{1}{2}$ mile
- Ⓑ about 1 mile
- Ⓒ about $1\frac{1}{2}$ miles
- Ⓓ about 2 miles

2. Sophia baby-sat for $3\frac{7}{12}$ hours on Friday. She baby-sat $2\frac{5}{8}$ hours on Saturday. Which is the **best** estimate of how many hours Sophia baby-sat altogether?

- Ⓐ about $5\frac{1}{2}$ hours
- Ⓑ about 6 hours
- Ⓒ about $6\frac{1}{2}$ hours
- Ⓓ about 7 hours

3. Three fences on a ranch measure $\frac{15}{16}$ mile, $\frac{7}{8}$ mile, and $\frac{7}{16}$ mile. Which is the **best** estimate of the total length of all three fences?

- Ⓐ $1\frac{1}{2}$ miles
- Ⓑ 2 miles
- Ⓒ $2\frac{1}{2}$ miles
- Ⓓ 3 miles

4. Mr. Krasa poured $\frac{5}{16}$ gallon of white paint into a bucket. He then added $\frac{3}{4}$ gallon of blue paint and $\frac{3}{8}$ gallon of red paint. Which is the **best** estimate of the total amount of paint in the bucket?

- Ⓐ $\frac{3}{4}$ gallon
- Ⓑ 1 gallon
- Ⓒ $1\frac{1}{2}$ gallons
- Ⓓ 3 gallons

5. Gina wants to ship three books that weigh $2\frac{7}{16}$ pounds, $1\frac{7}{8}$ pounds and $\frac{1}{2}$ pound. The maximum weight she can ship is 5 pounds. Estimate to see if Gina can ship all 3 books. Explain your answer.

Gina can ship all three books. I used the benchmarks

$\frac{1}{2}$ for $\frac{7}{16}$, 1 for $\frac{7}{8}$, and $\frac{1}{2}$ for $\frac{1}{2}$. Then I added $2\frac{1}{2} + 2 + \frac{1}{2} = 5$.

The estimated weight is 5 pounds.

Answer Key

Lesson 61
CC.5.NF.2

Name ______________________

1. Jacques caught 3 fish weighing a total of $23\frac{1}{2}$ pounds. Two of the fish weighed $9\frac{5}{8}$ and $6\frac{1}{4}$ pounds. How much did the third fish weigh?

   (A) $6\frac{3}{8}$ pounds
   (B) $7\frac{3}{8}$ pounds
   (C) $7\frac{5}{8}$ pounds
   (D) $8\frac{3}{8}$ pounds

2. Maria bought a total of $1\frac{3}{4}$ dozen bagels. Of the total, she bought $\frac{1}{6}$ dozen whole grain bagels, $\frac{3}{4}$ dozen sesame seed bagels, and some plain bagels. How many dozen plain bagels did Maria buy?

   (A) $\frac{5}{6}$ dozen
   (B) 1 dozen
   (C) $\frac{11}{12}$ dozen
   (D) $2\frac{2}{3}$ dozen

3. A squash, an apple, and an orange weigh a total of $2\frac{3}{8}$ pounds. The squash weighs $1\frac{15}{16}$ pounds, and the apple weighs $\frac{1}{4}$ pound. How much does the orange weigh?

   (A) $\frac{1}{8}$ pound
   (B) $\frac{3}{16}$ pound
   (C) $\frac{1}{4}$ pound
   (D) $\frac{5}{16}$ pound

4. Kelsey entered the triathlon at Camp Meadowlark. The total distance was $15\frac{11}{16}$ miles. The bike segment was $12\frac{1}{4}$ miles, and the running segment was $3\frac{1}{16}$ miles. How long was the swimming segment?

   (A) $\frac{3}{16}$ mile
   (B) $\frac{1}{4}$ mile
   (C) $\frac{5}{16}$ mile
   (D) $\frac{3}{8}$ mile

5. In three days this week, Julio worked $18\frac{7}{10}$ total hours. He worked $6\frac{1}{5}$ hours on the first day and $6\frac{2}{5}$ hours on the second day. Explain how you would find the number of hours Julio worked on the third day.

   I would add the first two days together: $6\frac{1}{5} + 6\frac{2}{5} = 12\frac{3}{5}$. I would rename $12\frac{3}{5}$ as $12\frac{6}{10}$ and then subtract $12\frac{6}{10}$ from $18\frac{7}{10}$: $18\frac{7}{10} - 12\frac{6}{10} = 6\frac{1}{10}$.

Lesson 62
CC.5.NF.3

Name ______________________

1. Taylor took 560 photographs during summer vacation. She placed 12 photos on each page of her scrapbook, except the last page. She had fewer than 12 photos to put on the last page. How many photos did Taylor place on the last page of the scrapbook?

   (A) 7
   (B) 8
   (C) 9
   (D) 10

2. Marla filled up her car's gas tank and then went on a trip. After she drove 329 miles, she filled her tank with 14 gallons of gas. If she drove the same number of miles on each gallon of gas, how many miles per gallon did Marla drive?

   (A) 23 miles per gallon
   (B) $23\frac{1}{2}$ miles per gallon
   (C) 24 miles per gallon
   (D) $24\frac{1}{2}$ miles per gallon

3. Kate made 180 ounces of punch for a party. She pours 8 ounces of punch for one serving. How many people can have a full serving?

   (A) 22
   (B) $22\frac{1}{2}$
   (C) 23
   (D) 25

4. The pool director has a list of 123 students who have signed up for swimming lessons. The pool director can register 7 students in each class. What is the **least** number of classes needed for all the students to be registered in a class?

   (A) 16
   (B) 17
   (C) 18
   (D) 19

5. Molly has a weekend job picking apples. She picked 1,078 apples last weekend and put them in bags that hold 12 apples each. How many bags containing exactly 12 apples each did Molly fill? Explain how you used the quotient and the remainder to answer the question.

   89 bags; Possible explanation: 1,078 ÷ 12 is 89 R 10. I used the quotient as the answer. I did not write the remainder as a fraction because the problem asks how many 12-apple bags Molly made and a 10-apple bag would be a fraction of a bag.

Lesson 63
CC.5.NF.3

Name ______________________

1. Four friends share 3 apples equally. What fraction of an apple does each friend get?

   (A) $\frac{2}{3}$
   (B) $\frac{3}{4}$
   (C) $1\frac{1}{4}$
   (D) $1\frac{1}{3}$

2. Ten pounds of rice are distributed equally into 6 bags to give out at the food bank. How many pounds of rice are in each bag?

   (A) $\frac{3}{5}$ pound
   (B) $1\frac{1}{3}$ pounds
   (C) $1\frac{2}{3}$ pounds
   (D) $1\frac{4}{5}$ pounds

3. Twelve friends share 4 pizzas equally. What fraction of a pizza does each friend get?

   (A) $\frac{1}{12}$
   (B) $\frac{1}{3}$
   (C) $\frac{1}{4}$
   (D) $\frac{1}{2}$

4. Terry picked 7 pounds of strawberries. She wants to share the strawberries equally among 3 of her neighbors. How many pounds of strawberries will each neighbor get?

   (A) $\frac{3}{7}$ pound
   (B) $\frac{7}{10}$ pound
   (C) $1\frac{3}{7}$ pounds
   (D) $2\frac{1}{3}$ pounds

5. Jake baked 5 cherry pies. He wants to share them equally among 3 of his neighbors. Jake says that each neighbor will get $\frac{3}{5}$ of a cherry pie. Do you agree? Support your answer.

   No, I disagree. Possible answer: Jake divided 3 pies among 5 people, 3 ÷ 5. To divide 5 pies among 3 people, you should write $5 \div 3 = 5 \times \frac{1}{3} = \frac{5}{3}$, or $1\frac{2}{3}$. Each neighbor will get $1\frac{2}{3}$ cherry pies.

Lesson 64
CC.5.NF.4a

Name ______________________

1. Sophie uses 18 beads to make a necklace. Three-sixths of the beads are purple. How many of Sophie's beads are purple?

   (A) 6
   (B) 9
   (C) 12
   (D) 15

2. Charlotte bought 16 songs. Three-fourths of the songs are pop songs.

   How many of the songs are pop songs?

   (A) 16
   (B) 12
   (C) 8
   (D) 4

3. Mr. Walton ordered 12 pizzas for the art class celebration. One-fourth of the pizzas had only mushrooms.

   How many of the pizzas had only mushrooms?

   (A) 3
   (B) 4
   (C) 8
   (D) 9

4. Trisha's mom baked 16 muffins. Two-eighths of the muffins have cranberries.

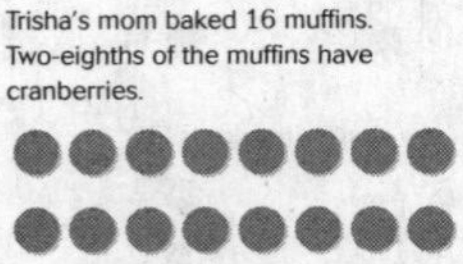

   How many of the muffins have cranberries?

   (A) 12
   (B) 8
   (C) 4
   (D) 2

5. Caleb took 24 photos at the zoo. Three-eighths of his photos are of giraffes. Explain how to use a model to find how many photos Caleb took of giraffes.

   Possible explanation: Draw 24 Xs to represent the photos. Arrange the Xs in 8 equal rows with 3 Xs in each row. So each row represents $\frac{1}{8}$ of the photos. Circle 3 rows to show $\frac{3}{8}$ of 24. There will be 9 Xs circled, so Caleb took 9 photos of giraffes.

Lesson 65
CC.5.NF.4a

Name _____

1. Gwen uses $\frac{2}{3}$ cup of sugar for one batch of cookies. She used a model to find how much sugar to use in 2 batches of cookies.

How much sugar does Gwen need for 2 batches of cookies?

Ⓐ $1\frac{1}{3}$ cups

Ⓑ $1\frac{2}{3}$ cups

Ⓒ $2\frac{1}{3}$ cups

Ⓓ $2\frac{2}{3}$ cups

2. Brandon used $\frac{3}{4}$ of an 8-ounce package of blueberries to make muffins. How many ounces of blueberries did he use for the muffins? You may use a model to help you solve the problem.

Ⓐ 2 ounces

Ⓑ 4 ounces

Ⓒ 6 ounces

Ⓓ $7\frac{1}{4}$ ounces

3. Yoshi wants $\frac{3}{5}$ of his garden to have red flowers. His garden has an area of 3 square yards. He used a model to find the area of his garden that will have red flowers.

What area of Yoshi's garden will have red flowers?

Ⓐ $1\frac{1}{5}$ square yards

Ⓑ $1\frac{4}{5}$ square yards

Ⓒ $2\frac{1}{5}$ square yards

Ⓓ $3\frac{3}{5}$ square yards

4. Kenya needs $\frac{1}{4}$ yard of material to make a placemat. How much material does she need for 6 placemats? You may use a model to help you solve the problem.

Ⓐ $1\frac{1}{4}$ yards

Ⓑ $1\frac{1}{2}$ yards

Ⓒ $1\frac{3}{4}$ yards

Ⓓ $6\frac{1}{4}$ yards

5. Mike has a 5-pound bag of apples. He will use $\frac{3}{4}$ of the bag to make pies. Explain how to use a model to find how many pounds of apples Mike will use for the pies.

Possible explanation: draw 5 circles to represent the 5 pounds of apples, and divide each circle into 4 equal parts. Shade 3 of the 4 parts of each circle so each circle shows $\frac{3}{4}$ of a whole. The shaded parts of the 5 circles show $\frac{15}{4}$, or $3\frac{3}{4}$, so Mike will use $3\frac{3}{4}$ pounds of apples.

Number and Operations–Fractions — 65

Lesson 66
CC.5.NF.4a

Name _____

1. Julia has a recipe for salad dressing that calls for $\frac{1}{4}$ cup of sugar. Julia is making 5 batches of the salad dressing. How much sugar will she use?

Ⓐ $\frac{4}{5}$ cup

Ⓑ $1\frac{1}{5}$ cups

Ⓒ $1\frac{1}{4}$ cups

Ⓓ $5\frac{1}{4}$ cups

2. Taniqua took a test that had 20 questions. She got $\frac{4}{5}$ of the questions correct. How many questions did Taniqua get correct?

Ⓐ 25

Ⓑ 16

Ⓒ 15

Ⓓ 12

3. In a class book order, $\frac{2}{3}$ of the books are fantasy and $\frac{1}{4}$ of the books are biography. If the order contains 60 books, how many books are either fantasy or biography?

Ⓐ 15

Ⓑ 30

Ⓒ 40

Ⓓ 55

4. Laurie runs around a track that is $\frac{1}{4}$ mile long. If she does 10 laps around the track, how far does she run?

Ⓐ $\frac{2}{5}$ mile

Ⓑ $2\frac{1}{4}$ miles

Ⓒ $2\frac{1}{2}$ miles

Ⓓ $10\frac{1}{4}$ miles

5. Mrs. Jackson asked Lance to explain to the class how to find the answer for $9 \times \frac{3}{4}$. How should Lance explain the steps to take to find the answer.

Possible explanation: first, write the whole number 9 as a fraction with a denominator of 1. The problem becomes $\frac{9}{1} \times \frac{3}{4}$. Then, multiply the numerators and multiply the denominators. The product of the numerators is $9 \times 3 = 27$, and the product of the denominators is $1 \times 4 = 4$, so $9 \times \frac{3}{4} = \frac{27}{4}$. Finally, write the product in simplest form by dividing the numerator by the denominator. 27 divided by 4 is $6\frac{3}{4}$.

66 — Number and Operations–Fractions

Lesson 67
CC.5.NF.4a

Name _____

1. Julia has a recipe for salad dressing that calls for $\frac{3}{4}$ cup of vegetable oil. How much vegetable oil should she use to make $\frac{1}{2}$ of the recipe for salad dressing?

Ⓐ $1\frac{1}{4}$ cups

Ⓑ $\frac{2}{3}$ cup

Ⓒ $\frac{1}{2}$ cup

Ⓓ $\frac{3}{8}$ cup

2. A scientist had $\frac{3}{4}$ liter of solution. He used $\frac{1}{6}$ of the solution for an experiment. How much solution did the scientist use for the experiment?

Ⓐ $\frac{1}{8}$ liter

Ⓑ $\frac{3}{8}$ liter

Ⓒ $\frac{1}{2}$ liter

Ⓓ $\frac{7}{12}$ liter

3. Of the flowers on Jill's front lawn, $\frac{2}{5}$ are tulips. Of the tulips, $\frac{5}{8}$ are yellow. What fraction of the flowers on Jill's front lawn are yellow tulips?

Ⓐ $\frac{7}{13}$

Ⓑ $\frac{1}{2}$

Ⓒ $\frac{1}{4}$

Ⓓ $\frac{1}{8}$

4. Otis bought a total of $\frac{7}{10}$ pound of grapes and cherries. The weight of the grapes is $\frac{2}{3}$ of the total weight. What is the weight of the grapes?

Ⓐ $\frac{3}{10}$ pound

Ⓑ $\frac{7}{15}$ pound

Ⓒ $\frac{9}{13}$ pound

Ⓓ $\frac{20}{21}$ pound

5. Marni and Leigh shared a pizza. Marni ate $\frac{4}{5}$ of $\frac{5}{12}$ of the pizza. Leigh ate $\frac{1}{2}$ of $\frac{2}{3}$ of the pizza. They both said that they ate the same amount of pizza. Do you agree? Support your answer.

Yes. Possible explanation: to find the amount of pizza each ate, I multiplied the fractions and wrote them in simplest form. Then, to find if they ate the same amount of pizza, I compared the products and found that they are the same: $\frac{4}{5} \times \frac{5}{12} = \frac{20}{60} = \frac{1}{3}$ and $\frac{2}{3} \times \frac{1}{2} = \frac{2}{6} = \frac{1}{3}$.

Number and Operations–Fractions — 67

Lesson 68
CC.5.NF.4b

Name _____

1. Marta breaded $\frac{1}{2}$ of the fish she cooked for dinner. She ate $\frac{1}{3}$ of the breaded fish. She used a model to find how much of the fish she had eaten.

How much of the fish did Marta eat?

Ⓐ $\frac{1}{6}$

Ⓑ $\frac{1}{5}$

Ⓒ $\frac{2}{5}$

Ⓓ $\frac{2}{3}$

2. Lawrence bought $\frac{2}{3}$ pound of roast beef. He used $\frac{3}{4}$ of it to make a sandwich. How much roast beef did Lawrence use for his sandwich? You may use a model to help you solve the problem.

Ⓐ $\frac{5}{12}$ pound

Ⓑ $\frac{1}{2}$ pound

Ⓒ $\frac{5}{7}$ pound

Ⓓ $\frac{6}{7}$ pound

3. Alexa planted tulips in $\frac{2}{5}$ of her garden. Of the tulips, $\frac{2}{3}$ are yellow tulips. She used a model to find what part of her garden has yellow tulips.

What part of Alexa's garden has yellow tulips?

Ⓐ $\frac{2}{15}$

Ⓒ $\frac{1}{3}$

Ⓑ $\frac{4}{15}$

Ⓓ $\frac{1}{2}$

4. A scientist has a bottle that is $\frac{5}{8}$ full of solution. He uses $\frac{2}{5}$ of the solution in the bottle for an experiment. How much of a full bottle of solution does he use? You may use a model to help you solve the problem.

Ⓐ $\frac{7}{13}$

Ⓑ $\frac{1}{2}$

Ⓒ $\frac{1}{4}$

Ⓓ $\frac{1}{40}$

5. Krista walks $\frac{3}{4}$ mile to school every day. So far today she has walked $\frac{1}{2}$ the distance to school. Explain how to use a model to find how far Krista has walked so far today.

Possible explanation: draw a rectangle and divide it into fourths. Shade $\frac{3}{4}$ of the rectangle. Then, divide each fourth into halves, and shade $\frac{1}{2}$ of each of the shaded fourths. Three out of 8 sections will be shaded twice. So, Krista has walked $\frac{3}{8}$ mile so far today.

68 — Number and Operations–Fractions

© Houghton Mifflin Harcourt Publishing Company

1. Ana has a poster that is $1\frac{2}{3}$ feet high and $2\frac{1}{4}$ feet wide. She used an area model to find the area of the poster.

	2	+	$\frac{1}{4}$
1			
$+$			
$\frac{2}{3}$			

What is the area of Ana's poster?

- (A) $3\frac{1}{2}$ square feet
- (B) $3\frac{3}{4}$ square feet
- (C) $3\frac{11}{12}$ square feet
- (D) $4\frac{1}{2}$ square feet

2. The top of Colin's desk is $2\frac{2}{3}$ feet long and $2\frac{1}{4}$ feet wide. What is the area of the top of Colin's desk? You may use an area model to help you.

- (A) $4\frac{1}{6}$ square feet
- (B) $4\frac{11}{12}$ square feet
- (C) $5\frac{11}{12}$ square feet
- (D) 6 square feet

3. Eloise is painting a mural that is $1\frac{3}{4}$ yards long and $1\frac{1}{4}$ yards high. She uses a grid to find the area of the mural.

What is the area of the mural?

- (A) $2\frac{3}{16}$ square yards
- (B) 6 square yards
- (C) $8\frac{3}{4}$ square yards
- (D) 35 square yards

4. A ping pong table is $2\frac{3}{4}$ meters long and $1\frac{1}{2}$ meters wide. What is the area of the ping pong table? You may use an area model to help you.

- (A) $4\frac{1}{8}$ square meters
- (B) $4\frac{1}{4}$ square meters
- (C) $4\frac{3}{8}$ square meters
- (D) $4\frac{2}{2}$ square meters

5. Devon is shopping for a rug for her living room. The rug she likes is $2\frac{1}{2}$ yards long and $1\frac{1}{2}$ yards wide. Explain how Devon can use a grid to find the area of the rug. **Possible explanation: use a grid where the length of each unit square represents $\frac{1}{2}$ yard. The area of each unit square will represent $\frac{1}{4}$ square yard. Since $2\frac{1}{2}$ is equal to $\frac{5}{2}$, and $1\frac{1}{2}$ is equal to $\frac{3}{2}$, draw a rectangle that is 5 units long and 3 units wide. The 15 unit squares represent $\frac{15}{4}$ square yards, or $3\frac{3}{4}$ square yards.**

1. Doreen lives $\frac{3}{4}$ mile from the library. If Sheila lives $\frac{1}{2}$ as far away as Doreen, which statement below is true?

- (A) Sheila lives closer to the library.
- (B) Doreen lives closer to the library.
- (C) Sheila lives twice as far from the library as Doreen.
- (D) They live the same distance from the library.

2. Mrs. Stephens wrote 4 statements on the board and asked the class which one was true. Which statement below is true?

- (A) $\frac{5}{6} \times \frac{5}{6}$ is equal to $\frac{5}{6}$.
- (B) $\frac{2}{3} \times \frac{1}{3}$ is less than $\frac{2}{3}$.
- (C) $\frac{7}{8} \times 8$ is less than $\frac{7}{8}$.
- (D) $\frac{3}{5} \times 5$ is greater than 5.

3. Nadia needs $\frac{3}{4}$ cup of orange juice for a punch recipe. She will double the recipe to make punch for a party. Which statement below is true?

- (A) She will be using the same amount of orange juice.
- (B) She will be using less orange juice.
- (C) She will be using more orange juice.
- (D) She will be using $\frac{3}{4}$ as much orange juice.

4. It took Mary Lou $\frac{5}{6}$ hour to write a report for her English class. It took Heather $\frac{9}{10}$ as much time to write her report as it took Mary Lou. Which statement below is true?

- (A) It took them both the same amount of time.
- (B) Mary Lou spent less time writing her book report than Heather.
- (C) Mary Lou spent more time writing her book report than Heather.
- (D) It took Heather twice as long to write her book report than it took Mary Lou to write her report.

5. Dwayne will multiply a recipe for brownies by 4. If the recipe calls for $\frac{1}{3}$ cup of oil, will he need more than or less than $\frac{1}{3}$ cup of oil to make all the brownies? Explain your answer. **He will need more than $\frac{1}{3}$ cup of oil. Possible explanation: multiplying by 4 is like adding $\frac{1}{3}$ four times, so the answer will be greater than $\frac{1}{3}$.**

1. Stuart rode his bicycle $6\frac{3}{5}$ miles last week. This week he rode $1\frac{1}{3}$ times as far as he rode last week. Which statement below is true?

- (A) He rode the same number of miles both weeks.
- (B) He rode fewer miles this week.
- (C) He rode more miles this week.
- (D) He rode twice as many miles this week.

2. Mrs. Thompson is buying $1\frac{3}{4}$ pounds of turkey and $\frac{3}{4}$ as much cheese as turkey at a deli. Which statement below is true?

- (A) She is buying the same amount of turkey and cheese.
- (B) She is buying less turkey than cheese.
- (C) She is buying twice as much turkey as cheese.
- (D) She is buying more turkey than cheese.

3. Miss Parks wrote 4 statements on the board and asked the class which one was true. Which statement below is true?

- (A) $3\frac{2}{3} \times \frac{4}{5}$ is greater than $3\frac{2}{3}$.
- (B) $1\frac{7}{8} \times 2\frac{1}{3}$ is greater than $2\frac{1}{3}$.
- (C) $2\frac{5}{6} \times \frac{8}{8}$ is less than $2\frac{5}{6}$.
- (D) $2\frac{3}{8} \times 4$ is less than 4.

4. Diana worked on her science project for $5\frac{1}{3}$ hours. Gabe worked on his science project $1\frac{1}{4}$ times as long as Diana. Which statement below is true?

- (A) Gabe spent more time on his science project than Diana did on hers.
- (B) Diana worked on her science project longer than Gabe worked on his.
- (C) Gabe worked on his science project twice as long as Diana worked on hers.
- (D) They both worked on their science projects the same amount of time.

5. Kyleigh has a recipe for punch that calls for $2\frac{1}{4}$ cups of sherbet. If she uses $1\frac{2}{3}$ of that amount, will she be using *more than*, *less than*, or the *same* amount of sherbet? Support your answer.

more than; Possible answer: the product of two numbers greater than 1 will be greater than either factor.

1. Louis wants to carpet the rectangular floor of his basement. The basement has an area of 864 square feet. The width of the basement is $\frac{2}{3}$ its length. What is the length of Louis's basement?

- (A) 24 feet
- (B) 36 feet
- (C) 48 feet
- (D) 576 feet

2. Sally painted a picture that has an area of 480 square inches. The length of the painting is $1\frac{1}{5}$ as long as it is wide. Which of the following could be the dimensions of Sally's painting?

- (A) 20 inches by 24 inches
- (B) 12 inches by 40 inches
- (C) 16 inches by 30 inches
- (D) 15 inches by 32 inches

3. A rectangular park has an area of 6 square miles. The width of the property is $\frac{3}{8}$ the length of the property. What is the width of the property?

- (A) $1\frac{1}{2}$ miles
- (B) $2\frac{1}{4}$ miles
- (C) 3 miles
- (D) 4 miles

4. A pool at a park takes up an area of 540 square yards. The length is $1\frac{2}{3}$ times as long as the width. Which of the following could be the dimensions of the pool?

- (A) 21 yards by 35 yards
- (B) 20 yards by 27 yards
- (C) 15 yards by 36 yards
- (D) 18 yards by 30 yards

5. Brianna has a rug that has an area of 24 square feet. The width of the rug is $\frac{2}{3}$ the length of the rug. Explain how you can find the length and the width of the rug.

Possible explanation: I can use the strategy guess, check, and revise. My first guess would be a length of 8 feet. The width would be $\frac{2}{3} \times 8 = \frac{16}{3}$ or $5\frac{1}{3}$ feet. The area would be $8 \times 5\frac{1}{3} = 42\frac{2}{3}$ square feet, which is more than 24 square feet. My second guess would be a length of 6 feet. The width would be $\frac{2}{3} \times 6 = \frac{12}{3}$ or 4 feet. The area would be $6 \times 4 = 24$ square feet, which is correct. So the length is 6 feet and the width is 4 feet.

1. Jared made $12\frac{3}{4}$ cups of snack mix for a party. His guests ate $\frac{2}{3}$ of the mix. How much snack mix did his guests eat?

   (A) $4\frac{5}{12}$ cups

   (A) $4\frac{1}{2}$ cups

   (C) $8\frac{1}{2}$ cups

   (D) $12\frac{5}{7}$ cups

2. Kayla walks $3\frac{7}{10}$ miles for exercise each day. What is the total number of miles she walks in 31 days?

   (A) $117\frac{4}{10}$ miles

   (B) $114\frac{7}{10}$ miles

   (C) $34\frac{7}{10}$ miles

   (D) $6\frac{4}{5}$ miles

3. Carlos has $7\frac{1}{2}$ acres of farmland. He uses $\frac{1}{3}$ of the acres to graze animals and $\frac{1}{5}$ of the acres to grow vegetables. How many acres does Carlos use for grazing animals or for growing vegetables?

   (A) $1\frac{1}{2}$ acres   (C) 4 acres

   (B) $2\frac{1}{2}$ acres   (D) $6\frac{29}{30}$ acres

4. The table shows how many hours some students worked on their math project.

   Math Project

Name	Hours Worked
Carl	$5\frac{1}{4}$
Sonia	$6\frac{1}{2}$
Tony	$5\frac{2}{3}$

   April worked $1\frac{1}{2}$ times as long on her math project as Carl. For how many hours did April work on her math project?

   (A) $5\frac{3}{8}$ hours   (C) $7\frac{1}{2}$ hours

   (B) $6\frac{1}{3}$ hours   (D) $7\frac{7}{8}$ hours

5. Jessica rides the bus $8\frac{4}{5}$ miles each day. Explain how to use the Distributive Property to find the total number of miles Jessica rides in 20 days.

   Possible explanation: I can rewrite the expression:

   $20 \times 8\frac{4}{5} = 20 \times (8 + \frac{4}{5})$. Then I would multiply each number in the

   parentheses by 20: $(20 \times 8) + (20 \times \frac{4}{5})$. Then I would find the products

   of each problem in the parentheses: $160 + 16$. Finally, I would

   add: $160 + 16 = 176$. So, Jessica rides the bus 176 miles in 20 days.

---

1. Olivia needs to find the number of $\frac{1}{3}$-cup servings in 2 cups of rice. She used the number line below to find $2 \div \frac{1}{3}$.

   How many $\frac{1}{3}$-cup servings of rice are in 2 cups of rice?

   (A) 2

   (B) 3

   (C) 5

   (D) 6

2. Kwami bought 8 yards of lanyard. He cut the lanyard into $\frac{1}{2}$-yard pieces. How many pieces of lanyard did Kwami make?

   (A) 2

   (B) 8

   (C) 16

   (D) 64

3. Chris divided $\frac{1}{2}$ pound of nails into 6 small bags with the same amount in each bag. He used fraction strips to find the weight of each bag.

   How much does each small bag weigh?

   (A) $\frac{1}{2}$ pound

   (B) $\frac{1}{3}$ pound

   (C) $\frac{1}{6}$ pound

   (D) $\frac{1}{12}$ pound

4. Josie filled a watering can with $\frac{1}{3}$ quart of water. She poured the same amount of water from the can onto each of 3 plants. How much water did Josie pour onto each plant?

   (A) $\frac{1}{9}$ quart

   (B) $2\frac{2}{3}$ quarts

   (C) 3 quarts

   (D) 9 quarts

5. Four athletes shared $\frac{1}{2}$ gallon of sports drink equally. Explain how to use fraction strips to find how much sports drink each athlete got.

   Possible explanation: show a 1 whole strip with a $\frac{1}{2}$-strip

   below it. Then find 4 fraction strips that fit exactly below

   the $\frac{1}{2}$-strip. Four $\frac{1}{8}$-strips will fit, so $\frac{1}{2} \div 4$ equals $\frac{1}{8}$. Each

   athlete gets $\frac{1}{8}$ gallon of sports drink.

---

1. Ben is making a recipe that calls for 5 cups of flour. He only has a $\frac{1}{2}$-cup measuring cup. How many times will Ben need to fill the $\frac{1}{2}$-cup measuring cup to get 5 cups of flour?

   (A) $\frac{2}{5}$

   (B) $2\frac{1}{2}$

   (C) 7

   (D) 10

2. Lily made 3 pounds of coleslaw for a picnic. Each serving of coleslaw is $\frac{1}{8}$ pound. How many $\frac{1}{8}$-pound servings of coleslaw are there?

   (A) $2\frac{2}{3}$

   (B) 12

   (C) 24

   (D) 32

3. Kyle shares 3 bananas with some friends. If each person gets $\frac{1}{2}$ of a banana, how many people can share Kyle's bananas?

   (A) 9

   (B) 6

   (C) $1\frac{1}{2}$

   (D) $\frac{1}{6}$

4. A 6-mile walking trail has a distance marker every $\frac{1}{3}$ mile, beginning at $\frac{1}{3}$ mile. How many distance markers are along the trail?

   (A) 2

   (B) 6

   (C) 9

   (D) 18

5. Aya made 2 pans of brownies to give to some families in her neighborhood. Each family will get $\frac{1}{4}$ of a pan. How many families will share Aya's brownies? Explain how to use a diagram to find your answer.

   8 families; possible explanation: I can draw

   2 rectangles, one for each pan of brownies. Then I can

   divide each pan into fourths and count how many

   fourths there are in all. There are 8 fourths, so

   8 families can share the brownies. $2 \div \frac{1}{4} = 2 \times 4 = 8$.

---

1. Samara solved $\frac{1}{5} \div 10$ by using a related multiplication sentence. Which multiplication sentence could she have used?

   (A) $5 \times 10 = 50$

   (B) $\frac{1}{5} \times 10 = 2$

   (C) $5 \times \frac{1}{10} = \frac{5}{10}$

   (D) $\frac{1}{5} \times \frac{1}{10} = \frac{1}{50}$

2. Jawan solved $8 \div \frac{1}{3}$ by using a related multiplication sentence. Which multiplication sentence could he have used?

   (A) $8 \times \frac{1}{3} = \frac{8}{3}$

   (B) $\frac{1}{8} \times \frac{1}{3} = \frac{1}{24}$

   (C) $8 \times 3 = 24$

   (D) $\frac{1}{8} \times 3 = \frac{3}{8}$

3. Annette has $\frac{1}{4}$ pound of cheese that she is going to cut into 3 chunks of the same size. What fraction of a pound of cheese will each chunk be?

   (A) $\frac{1}{12}$ pound

   (B) $\frac{1}{8}$ pound

   (C) $\frac{1}{2}$ pound

   (D) $\frac{3}{4}$ pound

4. Eli made 2 peanut butter and jelly sandwiches and cut each one into fourths. How many $\frac{1}{4}$-sandwich pieces did Eli have?

   (A) $\frac{1}{8}$

   (B) $2\frac{1}{4}$

   (C) 4

   (D) 8

5. Miss Becker asked her class to write a division expression using a whole number and a unit fraction that will have a quotient greater than its dividend. Cassie wrote $\frac{1}{2} \div 6$. Explain why Cassie is incorrect. Then give a correct expression.

   Possible explanation: Cassie's expression is equivalent

   to $\frac{1}{2} \times \frac{1}{6} = \frac{1}{12}$, and the quotient, $\frac{1}{12}$, is less than the

   dividend, $\frac{1}{2}$. The expression $6 \div \frac{1}{2}$ is equivalent to

   $6 \times 2 = 12$, and the quotient, 12, is greater than the

   dividend, 6.

Answer Key   **119**

Lesson 77
CC.5.NF.7c

1. Tina has $\frac{1}{2}$ quart of iced tea. She pours the same amount into each of 3 glasses. Which equation represents the fraction of a quart of iced tea, n, that is in each glass?

   (A) $\frac{1}{2} \div \frac{1}{3} = n$

   (B) $\frac{1}{2} \div 3 = n$

   (C) $3 \div \frac{1}{2} = n$

   (D) $3 \div 2 = n$

2. Lucy bought 9 yards of ribbon on a spool. She cut the ribbon into $\frac{1}{2}$-yard pieces. Which equation represents the number of pieces of ribbon, n, Lucy has now?

   (A) $9 \div \frac{1}{2} = n$

   (B) $\frac{1}{2} \div 9 = n$

   (C) $2 \div 9 = n$

   (D) $9 \div 2 = n$

3. Which situation can be represented by $6 \div \frac{1}{3}$?

   (A) Rita has a piece of ribbon that is $\frac{1}{3}$ foot long. She cuts it into 6 pieces, each having the same length. How many feet long is each piece of ribbon?

   (B) Rita has 6 pieces of ribbon. Each piece is $\frac{1}{3}$ foot long. How many feet of ribbon does Rita have in all?

   (C) Rita has a piece of ribbon that is 6 feet long. She cuts it into pieces that are $\frac{1}{3}$ foot long. How many pieces of ribbon does Rita have?

   (D) Rita has a piece of ribbon that is 6 feet long. She cuts it into 3 pieces. How many feet long is each piece of ribbon?

4. Mrs. Green wrote the following equation on the board. $2 \div \frac{1}{3} = n$. Scott wrote this situation to represent the equation: Lisa and Frank shared $\frac{1}{3}$ pound of cherries equally. What fractional part of a pound did each one get?

   Does Scott's situation represent the equation? Support you answer.

   No. Possible answer: Scott's story would be
   represented by $\frac{1}{3}$ divided by 2, that is, $\frac{1}{3}$ pound being
   divided equally between 2 people. The equation shows
   2 wholes divided into thirds. The situation might be:
   2 pounds of cherries need to be divided into $\frac{1}{3}$-pound
   packages. How many packages will there be?

Lesson 78
CC.5.MD.1

1. The first stop on a bus route is 4 miles from school. How many yards are in 4 miles?

   (A) 48 yards

   (B) 144 yards

   (C) 7,040 yards

   (D) 21,120 yards

2. Anoki bought 36 yards of fabric to make costumes for the school play. What is that length in inches?

   (A) 3 inches

   (B) 12 inches

   (C) 108 inches

   (D) 1,296 inches

3. Sarah is 53 inches tall. Sarah's brother Luke is 4 inches taller than she is. What is Luke's height in feet and inches?

   (A) 4 feet 7 inches

   (B) 4 feet 9 inches

   (C) 5 feet 7 inches

   (D) 5 feet 8 inches

4. The distance between a football field and a parking lot is 135 feet. What is that length in yards?

   (A) 36 yards

   (B) 45 yards

   (C) 405 yards

   (D) 1,620 yards

5. The distance between second and third bases on a regulation baseball field is 90 feet. Scott says he needs to multiply to find the number of yards between second and third bases. Do you agree? Support your answer.

   No, I disagree. Possible answer: when you convert from
   smaller units to larger units, you need to divide. Since
   1 yard = 3 feet, I would divide 90 by 3 to find the
   number of yards. $90 \div 3 = 30$, so the distance between
   second and third bases is 30 yards.

Lesson 79
CC.5.MD.1

1. Brian filled 72 glasses with apple juice for a school party. If each glass holds 1 cup of juice, how many quarts of apple juice did Brian use?

   (A) 9 quarts

   (B) 18 quarts

   (C) 36 quarts

   (D) 288 quarts

2. Mrs. Davis has 64 bottles of water. If each bottle holds 1 pint of water, how many gallons of water does Mrs. Davis have?

   (A) 4 gallons

   (B) 6 gallons

   (C) 8 gallons

   (D) 32 gallons

3. Isabel bought 3 bottles of liquid soap. Each bottle has 1 quart of soap in it. How many fluid ounces of liquid soap are in the 3 bottles that Isabel bought?

   (A) 16 fluid ounces

   (B) 32 fluid ounces

   (C) 72 fluid ounces

   (D) 96 fluid ounces

4. Mark filled 48 glasses with orange juice for a camp breakfast. If each glass holds 1 cup of juice, how many quarts of orange juice did Mark use?

   (A) 6 quarts

   (B) 12 quarts

   (C) 24 quarts

   (D) 192 quarts

5. Beth filled 32 jars with paint. Each jar holds 1 pint of paint. Beth found that she needed 4 gallons of paint to fill the jars by converting more than once. Describe how Beth converted from pints to gallons.

   Possible answer: Beth converted 32 pints to quarts by
   dividing by 2 since there are 2 pints in a quart. Then
   she divided 16 quarts by 4 since there are 4 quarts in a
   gallon.

Lesson 80
CC.5.MD.1

1. Students picked 576 ounces of apples to make apple cider. How many pounds of apples did they pick?

   (A) 16 pounds

   (B) 36 pounds

   (C) 48 pounds

   (D) 9,216 pounds

2. Keiko bought 3 pounds of fruit salad. How many ounces of fruit salad did Keiko buy?

   (A) 16 ounces

   (B) 32 ounces

   (C) 36 ounces

   (D) 48 ounces

3. A female elephant can weigh up to 8,000 pounds. What is this weight in tons?

   (A) 2 tons

   (B) 3 tons

   (C) 4 tons

   (D) 8 tons

4. A truck loaded with concrete weighs about 30 tons. What is this weight in pounds?

   (A) 30,000 pounds

   (B) 60,000 pounds

   (C) 300,000 pounds

   (D) 600,000 pounds

5. Seth bought 3 pounds of grapes. Maritza bought 50 ounces of grapes. Whose grapes weighed more? Explain how you know.

   Maritza's. Possible explanation: I converted 3 pounds to
   ounces by multiplying by 16 since there are 16 ounces
   in a pound. $16 \times 3 = 48$, so Seth's grapes weighed
   48 ounces, which is less than Maritza's 50 ounces of
   grapes.

Lesson 81
CC.5.MD.1

1. At the bulk food store, Stacey bought 7 pounds of nuts. She used 8 ounces of nuts in a recipe and then made small bags to use for snacks. If each small bag contained 4 ounces of nuts, how many small bags of nuts did Stacey make?

   (A) 15
   (B) 19
   (C) 26 ●
   (D) 29

2. Keisha is walking around a track that is 400 yards long. She has walked around the track 5 times so far. How many more yards does she need to walk around the track to do 2 miles?

   (A) 1,520 yards ●
   (B) 3,120 yards
   (C) 3,280 yards
   (D) 8,560 yards

3. Devon uses 64 inches of ribbon to make 1 bow. How many yards of ribbon does Devon need to make 9 bows?

   (A) 8 yards
   (B) 16 yards ●
   (C) 24 yards
   (D) 48 yards

4. Brandon bought a 5-gallon container of paint to paint his house. After he finished painting, he had 2 quarts of paint left over. How many quarts of paint did Brandon use?

   (A) 3 quarts
   (B) 8 quarts
   (C) 18 quarts ●
   (D) 23 quarts

5. Vincent needs 30 inches of wood to make a shelf. Vincent says he needs 15 feet of wood to make 6 shelves. Do you agree? Support your answer.

   Yes, I agree. Possible explanation: I multiplied 30 × 6
   to find the total number of inches of wood that Vincent
   needs: 30 × 6 = 180; there are 12 inches in 1 foot, so I
   divided 180 by 12 to find the total number of feet:
   180 ÷ 12 = 15

Measurement and Data   81

Lesson 82
CC.5.MD.1

1. Ed bought 3 liters of water, 2,750 milliliters of sports drink, and 2.25 liters of juice. Which statement is true?

   (A) Ed bought 50 milliliters more sports drink than juice.
   (B) Ed bought 1.25 liters more water than juice.
   (C) Ed bought 75 milliliters more water than juice.
   (D) Ed bought 250 milliliters more water than sports drink. ●

2. Roland's dog has a mass of 2,500 dekagrams. What is the dog's mass in kilograms?

   (A) 0.25 kilogram
   (B) 2.5 kilograms
   (C) 25 kilograms ●
   (D) 250 kilograms

3. Sofia bought 3.25 meters of fabric to make a costume. How many centimeters of fabric did she buy?

   (A) 0.325 centimeter
   (B) 3.25 centimeters
   (C) 32.5 centimeters
   (D) 325 centimeters ●

4. Lorena's backpack has a mass of 10,000 grams. What is the mass of Lorena's backpack in kilograms?

   (A) 1 kilogram
   (B) 10 kilograms ●
   (C) 100 kilograms
   (D) 1,000 kilograms

5. Richard can walk at a rate of 5 kilometers in an hour. Explain how to find how many meters Richard can walk in an hour. Then find how many meters he walks in an hour.

   Possible explanation: since a kilometer is a larger
   unit than a meter, multiply to change to smaller units.
   There are 1,000 meters in a kilometer. So, to change
   kilometers to meters, multiply 5 × 1,000, which is 5,000.
   So, Richard walks 5,000 meters in an hour.

82   **Measurement and Data**

Lesson 83
CC.5.MD.1

1. When it is full, a fish tank holds 15 gallons of water. Jordan is using a 1-pint container to fill the fish tank. How many times will he need to fill the 1-pint container to fill the fish tank?

   (A) 30
   (B) 60
   (C) 90
   (D) 120 ●

2. An art teacher has a roll of art paper 5 meters long. She needs to cut it into 1-decimeter long pieces for a collage project. How many 1-decimeter pieces can she cut from the roll of art paper?

   (A) 5
   (B) 50 ●
   (C) 500
   (D) 5,000

3. Mickey needs to cut pieces of ribbon that are each 1 meter long to tie onto balloons. If he has 8 pieces of ribbon that are each 1 dekameter long, how many 1-meter pieces of ribbon can he cut?

   (A) 80 ●
   (B) 800
   (C) 8,000
   (D) 80,000

4. The largest known carnivorous dinosaur, Spinosaurus, weighed about 18,000 pounds. How many tons did the Spinosaurus dinosaur weigh?

   (A) 9 tons ●
   (B) 18 tons
   (C) 36 tons
   (D) 90 tons

5. A Komodo dragon lizard can grow up to about 30 decimeters in length. Toni says that this is 300 centimeters. Do you agree? Explain how you can use a table to support your answer.

   Yes. Possible answer: a table can show the relationship
   between centimeters and decimeters. 1 decimeter equals
   10 centimeters, 2 decimeters equals 20 centimeters,
   3 decimeters equals 30 centimeters, and so on. The
   pattern shows to multiply the number of decimeters by
   10 to find the number of centimeters. So there are 300
   centimeters in 30 decimeters.

Measurement and Data   83

Lesson 84
CC.5.MD.1

1. The high school football game started at 7:15 P.M. and ended at 10:44 P.M. How long did the game last?

   (A) 2 hours 9 minutes
   (B) 2 hours 29 minutes
   (C) 3 hours 9 minutes
   (D) 3 hours 29 minutes ●

2. Betsy spent 26 days traveling in Europe. How many weeks and days did Betsy travel in Europe?

   (A) 2 weeks 6 days
   (B) 3 weeks 5 days ●
   (C) 4 weeks 2 days
   (D) 5 weeks 1 day

3. Students arrived at the science museum at 1:15 P.M. They stayed at the museum for 2 hours 51 minutes. What time did the students leave the museum?

   (A) 3:06 P.M.
   (B) 4:00 P.M.
   (C) 4:06 P.M. ●
   (D) 4:44 P.M.

4. It takes Kate 10 minutes to walk to the bus stop. How many seconds does it take her to walk to the bus stop?

   (A) 6,000 seconds
   (B) 600 seconds ●
   (C) 60 seconds
   (D) 6 seconds

5. The Diaz family arrived for breakfast at a diner at 8:45 A.M. They stayed at the diner for 1 hour 23 minutes. What time did the family leave the diner? Explain how you found your answer.

   10:08 A.M. Possible explanation: I know that 1 hour later
   than 8:45 A.M. is 9:45 A.M. To find 23 minutes after that,
   I think 15 of the 23 minutes takes me to the next hour,
   10:00 A.M. Then, 23 minutes minus 15 minutes equals
   8 minutes, so the family left at 10:08 A.M.

84   **Measurement and Data**

Answer Key

Lesson 85
CC.5.MD.2

Use the line plot for 1–2.

Maya measured the heights of the seedlings she was growing. She made a line plot to record the data.

Seedling Growth (in inches)

1. What was the total growth, in inches, of Maya's seedlings?

   (A) 3 inches   (C) 7 inches

   (B) $3\frac{1}{2}$ inches   (D) 10 inches

2. What was the average height, in inches, of the seedlings she measured?

   (A) $\frac{11}{16}$ inch   (C) $\frac{3}{4}$ inch

   (B) $\frac{7}{10}$ inch   (D) $\frac{7}{8}$ inch

5. Shia measured the thickness of the buttons in her collection. She graphed the results in a line plot.

   What steps could Shia use to find the average thickness of her buttons?

   Button Thicknesses (in inches)

   Shia could add the total for each thickness. Then she would add those amounts and divide by the number of buttons, 9.

Use the line plot for 3–4.

A builder is buying property where she can build new houses. The line plot shows the sizes of the lots for each house.

House Lots (in acres)

3. How many acres does the builder buy?

   (A) 3 acres   (C) 6 acres

   (B) 4 acres   (D) 12 acres

4. What is the average size of the lots?

   (A) $\frac{1}{12}$ acre   (C) $\frac{1}{4}$ acre

   (B) $\frac{1}{6}$ acre   (D) $\frac{1}{3}$ acre

Lesson 86
CC.5.MD.3

1. Koji is building a tower out of paper. He starts by making 2 congruent circular bases. He then makes 1 curved surface for the body of the tower. What three-dimensional figure does Koji build?

   (A) cone
   (B) cylinder
   (C) prism
   (D) sphere

2. Which of the following **best** classifies this solid figure?

   (A) triangular pyramid
   (B) triangular prism
   (C) square pyramid
   (D) square prism

3. Tanya drew this solid figure on her notebook.

   What solid figure did Tanya draw?

   (A) hexagonal prism
   (B) pentagonal prism
   (C) hexagonal pyramid
   (D) pentagonal pyramid

4. Min Soo is making solid figures in the shape of party hats. He starts by making 1 circular base. He then makes 1 curved surface for the figure. What three-dimensional figure does Min Soo make?

   (A) prism
   (B) sphere
   (C) cylinder
   (D) cone

5. Randi wants to draw three-dimensional figures whose lateral faces are all rectangles. She says she can draw prisms **and** pyramids. Do you agree? Support your answer.

   No; Possible answer: Randi cannot draw pyramids because a pyramid has lateral faces that are triangles, not rectangles. She can draw prisms since the lateral faces of prisms are rectangles.

Lesson 87
CC.5.MD.3a

1. Chase built a solid figure with unit cubes. How many unit cubes did he use for his figure?

   (A) 5
   (B) 6
   (C) 7
   (D) 8

2. Diana used more than one unit cube to build a figure. When she traced around the figure, she drew a square. What is the **least** number of unit cubes she could have used?

   (A) 1
   (B) 2
   (C) 4
   (D) 9

3. Ella placed some unit cubes on her desk as shown below. How many unit cubes did Ella use?

   (A) 5
   (B) 10
   (C) 15
   (D) 20

4. Henry stacked these unit cubes. How many unit cubes did Henry stack?

   (A) 6
   (B) 9
   (C) 12
   (D) 18

5. Kamal has 24 unit cubes. He says he can build 8 different rectangular prisms with the cubes. Do you agree? Support your answer.

   No. Possible answer: Kamal can build 6 different rectangular prisms with the cubes: $1 \times 1 \times 24$, $1 \times 2 \times 12$, $1 \times 3 \times 8$, $1 \times 4 \times 6$, $2 \times 3 \times 4$, $2 \times 2 \times 6$.

Lesson 88
CC.5.MD.3b

1. Cole stacked 1-foot cube-shaped boxes in a storage bin as shown. What is the volume of the space he filled?

   Each cube = 1 cu ft

   (A) 20 cu in.
   (B) 20 cu ft
   (C) 60 cu in.
   (D) 60 cu ft

2. A jeweler received a carton of boxes packed with gift boxes. The gift boxes were 2 inches long on each edge. If 12 boxes completely fill the carton, what is the volume of the carton?

   (A) 24 cu in.
   (B) 48 cu in.
   (C) 96 cu in.
   (D) 144 cu in.

3. Lindsay filled a box with 1-centimeter cubes. What is the volume of box?

   Each cube = 1 cu cm

   (A) 16 cu cm   (C) 64 cu cm
   (B) 16 cu m   (D) 64 cu m

4. Marina packed 36 1-inch cubes into this box. How many layers of cubes did Marina make?

   (A) 2   (C) 5
   (B) 3   (D) 6

5. Marcy used 1-inch blocks to build a cube whose edges are 3 inches long. Landon used 1-inch blocks to build a cube whose edges are 6 inches long. Landon says his cube has twice the volume of Marcy's cube. Is Landon correct? Support your answer.

   No. Possible answer: Marcy's cube will have 9 cubes in the bottom layer and 3 layers for a total of 27 cubes. Its volume is 27 cu in. Landon's cube will have a bottom layer of 36 cubes and 6 layers. Its volume is 216 cu in. 216 is not twice as much as 27.

Answer Key

Lesson 89
CC.5.MD.4

1. The volume of a box of coloring pencils is 250 cubic centimeters. Which is the best estimate of the volume of the box that the coloring pencils came packed in?

Coloring Pencils | Coloring Pencils
Coloring Pencils | Coloring Pencils
Coloring Pencils | Coloring Pencils

- (A) 750 cu cm
- (C) 7,500 cu cm
- (B) 3,750 cu cm
- (D) 75,000 cu cm

2. Joe packed boxes of staplers into a larger box. If the volume of each stapler box is 400 cubic centimeters, which is the best estimate for the volume of the box that Joe packed with staplers?

Stapler | Stapler
Stapler | Stapler

- (A) 800 cu cm
- (C) 4,000 cu cm
- (B) 2,000 cu cm
- (D) 8,000 cu cm

3. The volume of a pencil box is 80 cubic inches. Which is the best estimate of the volume of the box that the pencil boxes came packed in?

Pencil box | Pencil box | Pencil box
Pencil box | Pencil box | Pencil box
Pencil box | Pencil box | Pencil box
Pencil box | Pencil box | Pencil box

- (A) 9,600 cu in.
- (C) 960 cu in.
- (B) 3,840 cu in.
- (D) 384 cu in.

4. Joe packed tissue boxes into a larger box. If the volume of each tissue box is 90 cubic inches, which is the best estimate for the volume of the box that Joe packed with tissue boxes?

Tissue box | Tissue box
Tissue box | Tissue box

- (A) 360 cu in.
- (C) 720 cu in.
- (B) 540 cu in.
- (D) 1,080 cu in.

5. Janelle is trying to decide which of two shipping boxes has the greater volume. Explain how Janelle can compare the volumes of the shipping box using small boxes.

Possible explanation: Janelle could fill each shipping box with smaller boxes and see how many of the smaller boxes fit in each shipping box. The shipping box that holds a greater number of smaller boxes has the greater volume.

Lesson 90
CC.5.MD.5a

1. Claudine filled a box with smaller boxes shaped like cubes. What is the volume of the box Claudine filled?

4 in. / 5 in. / 6 in.

- (A) 15 cubic inches
- (B) 25 cubic inches
- (C) 100 cubic inches
- (D) 120 cubic inches

2. Luke keeps his art supplies in a shoe box that is 12 inches long, 7 inches wide, and 5 inches high. What is the volume of the shoe box?

- (A) 420 cubic inches
- (B) 358 cubic inches
- (C) 240 cubic inches
- (D) 24 cubic inches

3. Barbie stacked small cubes into a box until it was full. What is the volume of the box?

3 in. / 8 in. / 5 in.

- (A) 18 cubic inches
- (B) 40 cubic inches
- (C) 120 cubic inches
- (D) 158 cubic inches

4. A storage bin in the shape of a rectangular prism has a volume of 5,400 cubic inches. The base area of the storage bin is 450 square inches. What is the height of the storage bin?

- (A) 9 inches
- (B) 11 inches
- (C) 12 inches
- (D) 15 inches

5. Melissa wants to know the volume of a box that is 4 inches long, 2 inches wide, and 5 inches tall. Explain how Melissa can use cubes to find the volume of the box.

Possible explanation: Melissa can use 1-inch cubes to build a box that is 4 inches long, 2 inches wide, and 5 inches tall. She can count the cubes or multiply the area of the base, 8 square inches, and the height, 5 inches, to find the volume, which is 40 cubic inches.

Lesson 91
CC.5.MD.5b

1. Antonio found an antique chest in his grandfather's attic.

3 ft / 4 ft / 2 ft

What is the volume of the chest?

- (A) 6 cubic feet
- (C) 12 cubic feet
- (B) 9 cubic feet
- (D) 24 cubic feet

2. When Emma went to college, her mother packed up all her old skiing trophies into a box with the dimensions shown.

2 ft / 4 ft / 1 ft

What is the volume of the box?

- (A) 7 cubic feet
- (C) 9 cubic feet
- (B) 8 cubic feet
- (D) 10 cubic feet

3. Kristin keeps paper clips in a box that is the shape of a cube. Each edge of the cube is 3 inches. What is the volume of the cube?

- (A) 6 cubic inches
- (B) 9 cubic inches
- (C) 18 cubic inches
- (D) 27 cubic inches

4. Will moved a box of old newspapers from the back room of the library.

5 ft / 3 ft / 2 ft

What is the volume of the box?

- (A) 10 cubic feet
- (B) 15 cubic feet
- (C) 30 cubic feet
- (D) 40 cubic feet

5. Tom keeps sticky notes in a box that is the shape of a cube. Each edge of the box is 4 inches. Tom says that the volume of the cube is 16 cubic inches. Is Tom correct? Explain.

No. Possible answer: the length, the width, and the height of the box are all 4 inches because the box is in the shape of a cube. Tom forgot to multiply by one of the dimensions. The correct volume is 64 cubic inches.

Lesson 92
CC.5.MD.5b

1. Ben is filling a box that has the shape of a rectangular prism with 1-inch cubes. A layer of 7 rows with 8 cubes in each row filled the bottom of the box. The volume of the box is 224 cubic inches. How many layers of cubes can Ben fit in the box?

- (A) 2
- (C) 8
- (B) 4
- (D) 10

2. Mary bought a puzzle in a box that has a width of 3 inches, a length of 10 inches, and a height of 8 inches. She put it in a box that has a volume of 576 cubic inches so she could mail it with some other things. How many cubic inches of space were left in the box?

- (A) 816 cu in.
- (C) 336 cu in.
- (B) 597 cu in.
- (D) 240 cu in.

3. Sylvia can buy a blue box or a green box to store her markers. Both boxes have a base that measures 8 inches by 4 inches. The height of the blue box is 2 inches. The height of the green box is 1 inch. How much greater is the volume of the blue box than the green box?

- (A) 96 cu in.
- (C) 35 cu in.
- (B) 64 cu in.
- (D) 32 cu in.

4. Mr. McDonald is designing a cabinet to store sports equipment in the gym. The length and width of one design cannot be the same as the length or width of another design. He wants the cabinet to be 5 feet high with a volume of 60 cubic feet. How many different designs, all with whole number dimensions, can he make?

- (A) 2
- (C) 6
- (B) 3
- (D) 12

5. Margie is packing 108 small boxes into a large carton. The small boxes will fill all of the space inside the large carton. Each small box is 3 inches long, 2 inches wide, and 1 inch high. The width of the base and the height of the large carton are the same. The length of the base is less than 36 inches. All of the dimensions are whole numbers. Explain how to find possible dimensions for the large carton.

Possible explanation: the volume of each of the boxes is 6 cubic inches: $3 \times 2 \times 1$. There are 108 boxes, so the volume of the carton is 6×108, or 648 cubic inches. Make a table to find that if the width and the height could both be 6 inches, the length would be $648 \div (6 \times 6)$, or $648 \div 36 = 18$ inches. The dimensions of the carton could be 6 inches high, 6 inches wide, and 18 inches long.

Note: Other possible dimensions are: $9 \times 9 \times 8$ and $18 \times 18 \times 2$

Answer Key

123

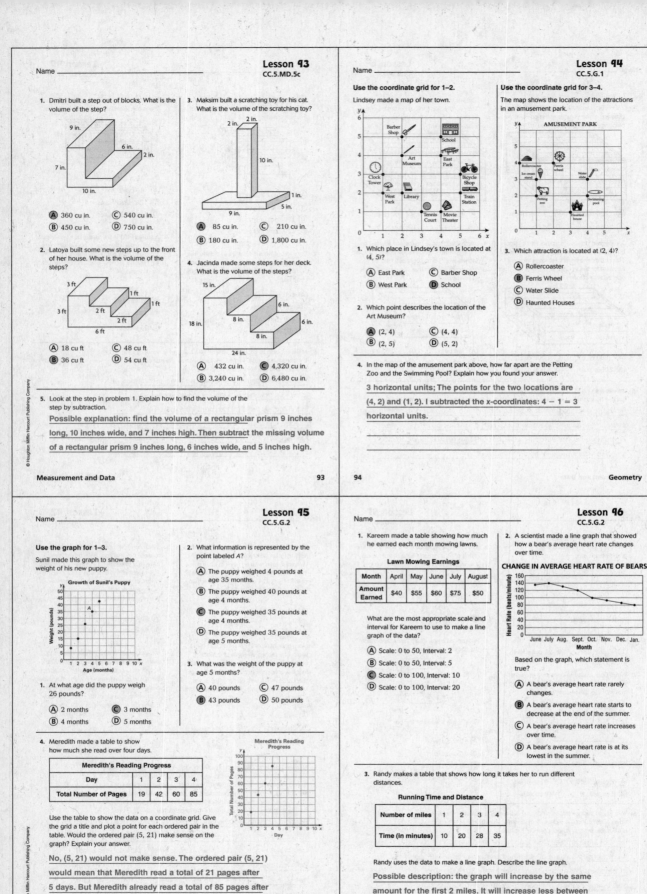

Lesson 93
CC.5.MD.5c

Name _____

1. Dmitri built a step out of blocks. What is the volume of the step?

9 in.
6 in.
2 in.
7 in.
10 in.

(A) 360 cu in.   (C) 540 cu in.
(B) 450 cu in.   (D) 750 cu in.

2. Latoya built some new steps up to the front of her house. What is the volume of the steps?

3 ft
1 ft
3 ft
2 ft
1 ft
2 ft
6 ft

(A) 18 cu ft   (C) 48 cu ft
(B) 36 cu ft   (D) 54 cu ft

3. Maksim built a scratching toy for his cat. What is the volume of the scratching toy?

2 in. 2 in.
10 in.
2 in.
1 in.
9 in.
5 in.

(A) 85 cu in.   (C) 210 cu in.
(B) 180 cu in.   (D) 1,800 cu in.

4. Jacinda made some steps for her deck. What is the volume of the steps?

15 in.
6 in.
18 in.
8 in.
6 in.
8 in.
24 in.

(A) 432 cu in.   (C) 4,320 cu in.
(B) 3,240 cu in.   (D) 6,480 cu in.

5. Look at the step in problem 1. Explain how to find the volume of the step by subtraction.

Possible explanation: find the volume of a rectangular prism 9 inches long, 10 inches wide, and 7 inches high. Then subtract the missing volume of a rectangular prism 9 inches long, 6 inches wide, and 5 inches high.

Measurement and Data   93

Lesson 94
CC.5.G.1

Name _____

Use the coordinate grid for 1–2.
Lindsey made a map of her town.

Use the coordinate grid for 3–4.
The map shows the location of the attractions in an amusement park.

1. Which place in Lindsey's town is located at (4, 5)?

(A) East Park   (C) Barber Shop
(B) West Park   (D) School

2. Which point describes the location of the Art Museum?

(A) (2, 4)   (C) (4, 4)
(B) (2, 5)   (D) (5, 2)

3. Which attraction is located at (2, 4)?

(A) Rollercoaster
(B) Ferris Wheel
(C) Water Slide
(D) Haunted Houses

4. In the map of the amusement park above, how far apart are the Petting Zoo and the Swimming Pool? Explain how you found your answer.

3 horizontal units; The points for the two locations are (4, 2) and (1, 2). I subtracted the x-coordinates: 4 − 1 = 3 horizontal units.

94   Geometry

Lesson 95
CC.5.G.2

Name _____

Use the graph for 1–3.
Sunil made this graph to show the weight of his new puppy.

Growth of Sunil's Puppy

1. At what age did the puppy weigh 26 pounds?

(A) 2 months   (C) 3 months
(B) 4 months   (D) 5 months

2. What information is represented by the point labeled A?

(A) The puppy weighed 4 pounds at age 35 months.
(B) The puppy weighed 40 pounds at age 4 months.
(C) The puppy weighed 35 pounds at age 4 months.
(D) The puppy weighed 35 pounds at age 5 months.

3. What was the weight of the puppy at age 5 months?

(A) 40 pounds   (C) 47 pounds
(B) 43 pounds   (D) 50 pounds

4. Meredith made a table to show how much she read over four days.

Meredith's Reading Progress				
Day	1	2	3	4
Total Number of Pages	19	42	60	85

Meredith's Reading Progress

Use the table to show the data on a coordinate grid. Give the grid a title and plot a point for each ordered pair in the table. Would the ordered pair (5, 21) make sense on the graph? Explain your answer.

No, (5, 21) would not make sense. The ordered pair (5, 21) would mean that Meredith read a total of 21 pages after 5 days. But Meredith already read a total of 85 pages after 4 days. The total after 5 days could not be less than 85.

Geometry   95

Lesson 96
CC.5.G.2

Name _____

1. Kareem made a table showing how much he earned each month mowing lawns.

Lawn Mowing Earnings				
Month	April	May	June	July	August
Amount Earned	$40	$55	$60	$75	$50

What are the most appropriate scale and interval for Kareem to use to make a line graph of the data?

(A) Scale: 0 to 50, Interval: 2
(B) Scale: 0 to 50, Interval: 5
(C) Scale: 0 to 100, Interval: 10
(D) Scale: 0 to 100, Interval: 20

2. A scientist made a line graph that showed how a bear's average heart rate changes over time.

CHANGE IN AVERAGE HEART RATE OF BEARS

Based on the graph, which statement is true?

(A) A bear's average heart rate rarely changes.
(B) A bear's average heart rate starts to decrease at the end of the summer.
(C) A bear's average heart rate increases over time.
(D) A bear's average heart rate is at its lowest in the summer.

3. Randy makes a table that shows how long it takes her to run different distances.

Running Time and Distance				
Number of miles	1	2	3	4
Time (in minutes)	10	20	28	35

Randy uses the data to make a line graph. Describe the line graph.

Possible description: the graph will increase by the same amount for the first 2 miles. It will increase less between 2 and 3 miles and still less between 3 and 4 miles.

96   Geometry

Lesson 97
CC.5.G.3

Name _____

1. Mr. Delgado sees this sign while he is driving.

   YIELD

   Which **best** describes the sign?

   Ⓐ triangle; regular polygon
   Ⓑ triangle; not a regular polygon
   Ⓒ hexagon; regular polygon
   Ⓓ hexagon; not a regular polygon

2. Mr. Diaz is building a fence around his yard. He drew a sketch of the fence line.

   Which **best** describes the fence line?

   Ⓐ pentagon; regular polygon
   Ⓑ pentagon; not a regular polygon
   Ⓒ hexagon; regular polygon
   Ⓓ hexagon; not a regular polygon

3. A stained glass window at the town library is the shape of a regular octagon. Which of the following describes a regular octagon?

   Ⓐ a figure with 6 congruent sides and 6 congruent angles
   Ⓑ a figure with 6 sides that are not congruent
   Ⓒ a figure with 8 sides that are not congruent
   Ⓓ a figure with 8 congruent sides and 8 congruent angles

4. Beth drew four quadrilaterals. Which of the quadrilaterals that she drew is a regular polygon?

   Ⓐ   Ⓒ
   Ⓑ   Ⓓ

5. Erica drew a rectangle and said that it Is a regular polygon because it has four congruent angles. Do you agree? Explain your answer.
   No, I disagree. Possible explanation: in a regular polygon, all sides are congruent and all angles are congruent. All the angles in a rectangle are right angles and congruent. All the sides are congruent only if the rectangle is a square. So Erica may have drawn a square that was regular polygon, but she also could have drawn a rectangle that did not have all sides congruent.

Geometry   97

Lesson 98
CC.5.G.3

Name _____

1. Which kind of triangle has no congruent sides?

   Ⓐ equilateral
   Ⓑ horizontal
   Ⓒ isosceles
   Ⓓ scalene

2. Nathan drew this triangle.

   Which of the following **best** classifies the triangle?

   Ⓐ scalene, acute
   Ⓑ scalene, obtuse
   Ⓒ isosceles, acute
   Ⓓ isosceles, obtuse

3. What is the **least** number of acute angles that a triangle can have?

   Ⓐ 0
   Ⓑ 1
   Ⓒ 2
   Ⓓ 3

4. Amanda drew this triangle.

   Which of the following **best** classifies the triangle?

   Ⓐ equilateral, acute
   Ⓑ isosceles, acute
   Ⓒ scalene, acute
   Ⓓ isosceles, right

5. Liza said that a triangle with exactly 2 congruent sides and a right angle is an acute isosceles triangle. Is she correct? Explain.
   No. Possible explanation: a triangle with a right angle is a right triangle. Since this triangle has exactly 2 congruent sides, it would be a right isosceles triangle.

98   **Geometry**

Lesson 99
CC.5.G.3

Name _____

1. Keiko drew the shapes of her tables on grid paper. Then she cut them out and used them on a floor plan to help arrange her furniture.

   Which two shapes that Keiko drew are congruent?

   Ⓐ A and B   Ⓒ B and C
   Ⓑ A and C   Ⓓ B and D

2. Ezra drew triangles to make this design.

   Which of the triangles appear to be congruent?

   Ⓐ A and B   Ⓒ C and E
   Ⓑ B and D   Ⓓ A and D

3. Fumiko drew the shapes of her neighbors' patios on grid paper.

   Which two shapes that Fumiko drew are congruent?

   Ⓐ A and B   Ⓒ B and C
   Ⓑ A and C   Ⓓ B and D

4. Ian drew triangles to make this design.

   Which of the triangles appear to be congruent?

   Ⓐ A and E   Ⓒ B and D
   Ⓑ B and C   Ⓓ C and E

5. Juanita has a quadrilateral that she thinks is a rhombus, but she does not have a ruler to measure the sides. How can Juanita determine whether the quadrilateral is a rhombus?
   Possible answer: she can fold the quadrilateral twice along the diagonals. If the sides match up, all four sides are congruent, making it a rhombus.

Geometry   99

Lesson 100
CC.5.G.4

Name _____

1. Jim's vegetable garden looks like this quadrilateral.

   What type of quadrilateral is it?

   Ⓐ trapezoid
   Ⓑ square
   Ⓒ rhombus
   Ⓓ rectangle

2. Cathy drew a picture of her backyard.

   What type of quadrilateral is Cathy's backyard?

   Ⓐ rectangle
   Ⓑ square
   Ⓒ rhombus
   Ⓓ trapezoid

3. The patio at the front of the school is a quadrilateral with 4 right angles and 4 congruent sides. What type of quadrilateral is it?

   Ⓐ trapezoid
   Ⓑ square
   Ⓒ rhombus
   Ⓓ rectangle

4. Tim's bedroom is shaped like this quadrilateral.

   What type of quadrilateral is it?

   Ⓐ rectangle
   Ⓑ square
   Ⓒ rhombus
   Ⓓ trapezoid

5. Gabrielle drew a quadrilateral with 3 congruent sides. She claims that it must be a rhombus or a square. Is she correct? Explain your answer.
   No. Possible explanation: the quadrilateral could be a rhombus or a square because both have at least 3 congruent sides, but, it could also be a trapezoid or a quadrilateral that is not a parallelogram.

100   **Geometry**

Answer Key